Written by the **Master Coach YLICH TARAZONA**

SERIES: Applied NLP, Influence, Persuasion, Suggestion and Hypnosis - Volume 1 of 3

The Power of HYPNOSIS

Theoretical-Practical Manual of Training in HYPNOSIS
And the Development of Persuasive Hypnotic Skills

*Extraordinary **Book** on **General Principles** of **MODERN HYPNOSIS, TRANCE and PHENOMENA HYPNOTIC, ERICKSONIAN HYPNOSIS and FREUDIAN, SUGGESTIONS and HYPNOTIC INDUCTIONS, CONVERSATIONAL HYPNOSIS, PATTERNS SHOW PERSUASIVE HYPNOTIC and HYPNOSIS SHOW** which will help you to understand and master this wonderful masterful art of HYPNOSIS in a fantastic journey of theoretical-practical training and learning, together* **with the most advanced modern methodologies, the most effective techniques and strategies will finally allow let you take this skill to the next level.**

In this BOOK in your SPECIAL EDITION you will learn to:

- BioReprogram your conscious and subconscious mind through Modern Methodologies and the Most Effective Techniques of Applied HYPNOSIS.
- Allow an optimal configuration of potentializing beliefs and dominate the suggestive inductions, as well as suggestions and hypnotic patterns more effective that allow you to consolidate your capacity to generate trances and hypnotic phenomena of high level in your coaching sessions, hypnotherapy sessions and show Hypnotic show in your audience and general public.
- Promote the flexibility of tactical-strategic thinking, and the understanding of the mental and psychological processes in the holistic dynamic between the mind (Neuro), the language (Linguistics), and the interaction between both (Programming), which allows you the correct use of HYPNOSIS and PERSUASION together with the tools of Applied NLP and Mental Reengineering to reinforce your learning and training.
- Have a clear and defined Action Plan, step by step, that allows you to develop the HYPNOTIC and PERSUASIVE SKILLS necessary to reach new desired hypnotic trance states (mental, emotional and psychological).
- Increase your POWER CIRCLE and your Level of Strength or Authority Level to a SUPERIOR LEVEL (FP's) that allow you to develop your hypnotic abilities and create orders, inductions and suggestions in a more optimal and effective way.

3rd Special Edition, Revised, Updated and Extended *(Includes Exercises and Action Plan)*

Transformational Coach

Writer and International Speaker

YES, you can learn to HYPNOTIZE, any person, at anytime and anywhere. The issue is not, if you enter into HYPNOSIS, the question is, when you enter. Since every person is HYPNOTIZABLE if you know the "HOW" and the "WHO" answer.

Theoretical-Practical Manual of Training in HYPNOSIS
And the Development of Persuasive Hypnotic Skills
Written by the **Master Coach YLICH TARAZONA**

3rd Special Edition Revised and updated by: Ylich Tarazona November 2017.
Cover Design and development by: Ylich Tarazona
Kindle eBook **ASIN: B076G97F14** / Paperback Kindle **ASIN: 154997100X**

ISBN-13: 978-1979740036
ISBN-10: 1979740038
SEAL: Independently Published ©

BISAC: Hypnotism / Hypnosis / Self Hypnosis / Hypnotherapy / Hypnosis
YLICH TARAZONA the right to be identified as the author of this work has been
affirmed by SafeCreative.org, Registration Code: **1710184603711**, in accordance with the
Copyright Worldwide. **Publication Date:** *October 18, 2017.*

Theoretical-Practical Manual of Training in HYPNOSIS
And the Development of Persuasive Hypnotic Skills
Written by the **Master Coach YLICH TARAZONA**

MENTAL reengineering PNL It is a virtual community for entrepreneurs. One of the Internet Website dedicated to providing COACHING in consolidating Skills and Development of Human Potential Maximum. Specialists in training, education and training of high level through NLP or Neuro Linguistic Programming, specializing in the supply of training and courses to achieve goals, objectives and consolidate effective Flesh results optimal performance; through a series of books, EBook's, Audios, Podcasters, Tele-Seminars Online, Audio-Visual Workshops, Webinars and Conferences Master of attending classes.

You cannot pretend to be associated with YLICH TARAZONA & MENTAL reengineering PNL in any form or use our name in connection with your own personal or professional practice, unless you are properly trained and certified validates that it proves that formally trained, properly trained or trained with us.

3rd Special Edition Revised and updated by: Ylich Tarazona November 2017.
Cover Design and development by: Ylich Tarazona
Kindle eBook **ASIN: B076G97F14** / Paperback Kindle **ASIN: 154997100X**

ISBN-13: 978-1979740036
ISBN-10: 1979740038
SEAL: Independently Published ©

BISAC: Hypnotism / Hypnosis / Self Hypnosis / Hypnotherapy / Hypnosis
Registration code: **1710184603711** / *License: All Rights Reserved © by SafeCreative.org / Intellectual Property Registration Date: 18-Oct-2017.*

<u>CONTRIBUTORS</u>:
Mariam Charytin Murillo Velazco
Ylich Leavitt Gabriel Peña Smith Tarazona
Jeffry Samuel Peña Tarazona
Genesis Zarahemla Odaylich Tarazona Maldonado

You can also contact the author directly via e-mail by:
MásterCoach.YlichTarazona@gmail.com

DEDICATION

Dedicated especially for you "APPRENTICE"

The content of this present book "**THE POWER OF HYPNOSIS - Theoretical and Practical Manual Training in Hypnosis and Hypnotic Persuasive Skills Development ©-® **". We provide the tools you require to start developing your hypnotic skills to the next level.

And this is my intention for you ...

Your friend **Coach Ylich Tarazona**

INTRODUCTION

<u>Relevant information for this edition.</u>

Hello such, my dear readers. First of all, thanks for purchasing this extraordinary book Hypnosis and hypnotism, I wrote thinking of you.

Before we begin, I want to communicate some essential changes I have made in this 3rd Special Edition. If you have some of my previous versions; You will see that I have made some revisions and important updates in the latest editions, as I seemed necessary to achieve fulfill the purpose for which I wrote this book for you. Among the changes I have made, I have incorporated a number of examples and practical exercises related to the lesson of some of the most relevant chapters. In the few cases where edit the text or change some content, they have been to adapt better examples and exercises recently incorporated in the present work.

These changes are almost imperceptible in most cases, since first of all I wanted to respect the original manuscript and the main idea of this book with its flaws and virtues. So, in the few occasions when I have incorporated some ideas, I've added some extra point or I added some elements of interest to my readers and learners, it is because I found convenient or necessary and vital to the proper application the principles of "**Modern hypnosis, trance and hypnotic phenomena, ericksoniana and Freudian hypnosis, suggestions and hypnotic inductions, conversational hypnosis**, Persuasive and hypnotic patterns show hypnosis show" Contained in this special edition.

> *If you had the opportunity to read some of my other printed or digital books, you have seen that both the literary style of my writing; and typographic characteristic style that I use when translating my ideas, seek a single purpose. Help you develop your full human potential to the next level, and allow a better understanding of the concepts, definitions and action plan that I share with all of you in order to help them internalize these vital and essential principles to your own life.*

To achieve this goal; at the end of some key chapters, I share a range of exercises that allow you to implement the essence of what you just studied. Likewise, I also offer them a series of summations or to reflect basic principles that will help you reinforce what you've learned.

Thus, champions and champions at the end of the book you will have real strategies, techniques, tools and effective methodologies that have been studied and tested over the years by the greatest experts in the field. Likewise, these principles have been implemented and put into action again and again by the same author, both as in their sections, shows and both virtual lectures and face parsonal level, with thousands of people who have applied these principles effectively to their own lives.

Such procedures have been routinely incorporated into this ADVANCED COURSE to guarantee optimal results by MODELS effective NLP or NLP APPLIED hypnosis and persuasion that have been checked through the years by the most renowned experts. Thus, avoiding the use of guesswork or simple theories.

For this reason, apprentice and dear readers, I'll give you some advice: Connect with the essence of this book, ACTIVELY LEE, every word, every line, every paragraph, every page, every chapter, every idea, every teaching, every example, every story, every exercise, every principle that love with all of you, and see how; gradually, step by step, line by line and precept upon precepts begin to have the excellent results required in each and every one of the most important and essential aspects of his life.

This course my dear readers is a powerful theoretical and practical for those who want to learn to develop effective tool hypnotic qualities. Of course, this book is not the only way to learn hypnosis. However, if you follow the directions step by step I in this book, and have the right attitude and the confidence, determination and commitment can assure you apply these principles in anyone.

It is important to note at this point that hypnotic skills you'll learn in this course ADVANCED involve a lot of responsibility and professional ethics. Always keep in mind that the correct application of hypnosis can be properly used, either for fun healthily and produce some laughter in our environment at some Hypnotic Show "or" we can also use hypnosis properly in therapeutic areas to generate large and extraordinary mental and emotional psychological changes in people in our coaching sessions or hypnotherapy. With this in mind, I want you to understand that this book gives you the information and resources needed in both cases to use hypnosis professionally and ethically especially so to ensure the welfare of all those involved in it. The use you give you will depend on your choice, but remember whatever purpose you want to achieve, you should always be based on the highest standards of professional ethics and decency, built on the principles and the highest moral values.

*YOU IMAGINE all you can accomplish get to learn apply these universal laws of success in your own life. You can imagine how your life would change dramatically for the better, to be able to conquer all fondest your dreams, goals and objectives you set out to achieve in this life, thanks to these **basic principles for success.** NOW POSSIBLE!*

LITERARY AND MY STYLE WORKS TYPOGRAPHIC

The teachings containing my books and courses mostly, are a strategic combination mixed with powerful metaphors, parables, allegories, illustrations, stories, quotes and quotations that have been collecting and summarizing during the years from different sources; such as books and works of various authors (to which, granted them all the credit and recognition they deserve for their valuable contributions).

The objective of extracting extraordinary collection of these great and renowned writers and translate them into my works is; help them better understand my readers, I want to convey information subjectively. In this way; through learning of symbolic and figurative representations, you my friends to acquire the main ideas.

So; my books, through their quotes, famous quotes, thoughts, stories, reflections and illustrative narratives can become a source of inspiration to help those individuals with full purpose of heart they want to change and transform their lives continuously and permanently.

Another of the Typographical I use to write my work methodologies; It is to use different literary styles, introducing a variety of punctuation, bold, italic, underlined, letter case combinations, among other conscious repetitions of ideas and teachings transmitted several times; again, and again, but in different contexts and situations, to record them in your conscious and subconscious mind. As well as sometimes "strategically change the way you write and express my ideas intentionally first, second and third person" lie I transmit information, in order to make the most didactic, versatile and pleasant reading for all my readers.

Should this seem inappropriate or wrong at some point for some of my readers, I want overtake them in advance that it is not in any way an oversight on my part, or lack of editing and transcription of the work. On the contrary, it has a clear objective and pursues a particular purpose. TRUST ME. It has a purpose for you, keep reading and you'll understand what I mean.

In another order of idea; Importantly also incorporated in the course of the book a wide variety of famous quotes, inspirational quotes scripture, Bible verses, philosophical concepts, examples, similes, exhibitions, descriptions and figured in the course of the whole work language. Since such expressions, concepts and ideas are able to subjectively stimulate a variety of sensations MULTI-SENSORY at both (visual, auditory and kinesthetic) that allow evoke images, sounds, sensations and emotions in the reader's mind.

Following the same order of idea; I include in all my works a series of positive statements, self-statements empowering, based on META-MODELS strategic NLP through a series of hypnotic commands and persuasive patterns that allow the reader to incorporate these suggestions and Subliminal inductions your mind conscious and subconscious, and producing them radically positive changes in their mental and psychological structure, creating in new neural connections more empowering.

And finally, APPRENTICE, among other resources I use are personal expressions like you and IT, to refer directly to my readers, with the sole intention that they can feel identified with my words, and have the full assurance and conviction that all I write my books thinking about them.

In the audible versions, such as in cases of audiobooks, podcasters, the Webminars, the Tele-Seminars and Online Conferences I use instrumental background music with sounds of nature, and at times binaural waves at different frequencies. To induce certain positive states in the brain. Among the many benefits offered by these powerful tools it is conducive to accelerated learning, conscious reflection, proper assimilation of ideas, mental alertness, stimulation of creativity, relaxation, concentration and meditation among many other advantages. As they have shown in numerous studies on the subject. Including the doctoral thesis Pedro, *which we report excellent and wonderful positive effects of these sounds, both psychological and physiological.*

The purpose of introducing this range of literary, typographic styles; METAPHORICAL and binaural (the latter only in cases Audible), merged with a varied set of techniques NLP or Neuro Linguistic Programming Applied Reengineering beginning Cerebral Neuro-Coaching autohypnosis among other tools. It is to enable my readers receive a transformational education more useful, holistic and comprehensive, enabling them to embrace new ideas, thus avoiding the slightest resistance to change, and creating a greater psychological impact - emotional in the retention process - learning.

******IMPORTANT******

This book in its special edition is a transcription adapted from Podcasters, Webminars, teleseminar, online course and face Conference Coach Ylich Tarazona entitled "THE POWER OF HYPNOSIS - **Theoretical and Practical Manual Training in Hypnosis and Hypnotic Persuasive Skills Development** © ® ". *For* that reason; this book reflects a unique and original style of transcription. Since it is an adaptation of a work Audio and Video Course Conference; rather than a literary work, written as such.

TABLE OF CONTENTS

CHAPTER I: PRINCIPLES OF HYPNOSIS AND THROUGH HYPNOTIC SUGGESTION HISTORY

Part One: Brief History of Hypnosis

Hello such, champions and champions this particular book is special to me, since hypnosis and suggestion are one of the tools and methodologies of the most powerful communication that struck me when I started my way in the study of this wonderful art NLP, Neuro Coaching, Reengineering Brain and bioprogramming. Therefore, I want to share with you all this knowledge simply, entering in this fascinating and yet so complex subject simple but effective way.

> A good way to introduce this wonderful world of hypnosis, is transit through its history through the centuries. Thus, you and me together traveling through time, we will understand more about this phenomenon. And therefore, we will be better able to understand it, understand it and apply it. I propose; therefore, we give a brief historical journey that will help us to contextualize hypnosis and all aspects related to it.

To begin, we can say that hypnosis like suggestion is as old; as humanity itself, ie there since the early origins of human history, when humans were reported. The ancient Sumerians, Egyptians and Babylonians practiced, getting what they considered "miracle cures" through it. Importantly, of course, that ANTIGUA HYPNOSIS has evolved, and has had many "practical ways" and many "old names" throughout the whole story. Subsequently, this esoteric and therapeutic component was evolving and developing in practice as we know it today. Although it is not possible to fix the exact moment of history in which there was this discovery,

> *Apprentice, the art of ancient HYPNOSIS, was a mystic and progressive therapeutic process, which was developed and gradually evolved through the years, through a long and expensive journey, probably with details and errors, successes and failures, myths and realities, speculation and success, until our days.*

Nobody knows for sure the origins of mental suggestion and the former HYPNOSIS. Because, since the beginning of human history, there are many indications that men of all civilizations and primitive cultures used suggestive hypnotic procedures purposes many mystical, magical, healing, esoteric as therapeutic including in relieving pain, as well as certain psychic-mental and spiritual disorders.

Hypnosis and hypnotic suggestion in its many variations, has been used by various ancient cultures through the years. Many ancient nations used such practices among its rituals. Known today as states of "hypnotic trance" which are described in hieroglyphics, scrolls, plates and hundreds of other writings since ancient times.

In non-Western cultures ANTIGUA HYPNOSIS was used mainly by the "healers", "witch", "shamans" or "priests" being generally they (the healers and sorcerers) who entered into a trance as part of healing ceremonies and purification. Moreover, the ancient peoples like the Maya, Aztecs, Persians, Greeks, Egyptians and Sumerians also used hypnosis as a means of healing. Foremost among the (priests and shamans) that they caused a state of trance called "Magic Dream" through the laying on of hands, offering to the gods and ancestors, as well as other ritual songs and dances characterized by a monotonous rhythm.

Hypnotic suggestion and hypnosis is an old science studied and used in the service of humanity. For example: The ancient Egyptians about 4,500 years ago called HEALING SLEEP was a state very similar to the "Magic Dream" trance. Mainly in the larger more advanced civilizations such as the Sumerian nations, Egyptian, Babylonian and Greek used the HYPNOSIS different purposes both medical, curative and healing.

Apprentice, as we have learned in the preceding paragraphs hypnosis and suggestion have existed throughout history. Among the civilizations which it has historical record found in the use of this type of mental and psychic abilities, we can find the aforementioned ancient Sumerians, Babylonians, Syrians, ancient magicians Persians, Greeks and Egyptian priests (which were the most advanced civilizations in the use of these practices to ancient times), some of the teachers and Chinese monks, Buddhists, Tibetan and Hindu (who practiced a kind of meditation, which made them enter a state of deep trance) as well as various healers and magicians of ancient African civilizations (who were mostly those who entered a trance)

> This science in its infancy, as we have been studying throughout its history, was reserved and secretly practiced by very few. And clandestine and esoterically transmitted between ancient civilizations over time, thus creating, many taboos, myths and speculations around. Since many of these ancient cultures erroneously attributed their effects to divine powers, mystical, esoteric and even supernatural.

As we have learned so far apprentice, the first manifestations of the HYPNOSIS occurred in the past, in the form of self-hypnosis and hypnotic suggestions among primitive men of old, who, with his mysterious chants, their ritualistic dances monotonous rhythms, his passes enigmatic, keywords and invocations to the gods and ancestors, made of ancient HYPNOSIS a series of spells related to alleged magical, mystical and miraculous powers. Thus, they came to desensitize collectively sometimes with provocation infused pain (as in cases of trances in ancient and modern civilizations of the African tribes where you get to cataleptic and catatonic hypnotic states through their magical rituals).

Other characteristic features of ancient HYPNOSIS were believed to have visions and spiritual manifestations (EPIPHANY) where to enter these mystical states dominated fatigue or "magical dream," which allowed the cure of functional disorders including both mental healing and spiritual. In fact, this was the beginning of magic, the emergence of healers, sorcerers, shamans, healers and the introduction of priest craft who exercised great influence over the tribe or ancient civilizations. These being the cause of many of the myths, taboos, speculations and falsehoods still exist today around the practice of modern hypnosis.

As we have come to apprentice we have thousands of years ago. The ancient Sumerians, Egyptians and Babylonians realized that hypnosis was a tremendously powerful weapon wielded power and great influence, which allowed them to unleash amazing huge forces in the subconscious minds of his subjects. Naturally, they wanted to have that power hidden just under his absolute control, so surrounding the HYPNOSIS of "magic" and a series of rituals and occultism. Those sorcerers, magicians, sorcerers, shamans and ancient priests knew that people often resist the "simple explanations" and generally considered more certain, mystical and mysterious the most complicated and difficult explanations, so they surrounded the hypnosis of all those theatrics.

That apprentice reason, when those sorcerers, magicians, sorcerers, shamans and priests practiced ANTIGUA HYPNOSIS, performing strange rituals full of symbolisms, songs, magic circles, enigmatic passes, keywords and invocations to the gods and ancestors, as well as the use of candles, incense, strange sounds, among other things. And all those theatrics and drama whose only purpose, and the purpose was to keep hypnosis as something occult, mystical, esoteric and magical, out of reach of ordinary people, ie of his subjects. Since they noticed than those gullible people who witnessed those rituals assumptions believed that supposedly supernatural power of ancient HYPNOSIS was that healed them, it was those who gave them healing through those "complex rituals" those "invocations to the gods" and those drawings "mystical", canticles and symbolism. When was the mental suggestion of the person that took effect and (sorcerers, magicians, sorcerers, shamans and priests knew well) actually own? They understood very well, it was the patient's own mind performing healing, through the suggestive power of ancient hypnosis. And that exactly the same apprentice way, is what happens today more than 4,000 years later, hundreds of alleged hypnotists clinical and modern hypnotists as well as hundreds of hypnotists of theater or show of shows continue to maintain hypnosis as something occult, mystical and esoteric, consequently resulting in the large number of taboos, myths,

WHAT NOW APPRENTICE, now you can understand why there is so much confusion surrounding hypnosis? If hypnosis is real because then there is so much speculation, myths and falsehoods about him? ... Now you can understand where all these speculations came, myths and falsehoods that exist to this day? ... The purpose of this book is clearly teaching all the historical evolution of hypnosis, as I have done so far. My goal with this work is to show that hypnosis is real; but like many other ancient practices, this came to our days with many misrepresentations. And my intention is clarifying all those doubts, refute all these lies and clear yourself uncertainties, as also prove its effectiveness, introduce yourself medical tests - scientific,

So, without further ado, my dear readers continue ...

Before continuing apprentice, and go clarifying the matter and bring more light on this issue, I consider it appropriate and important to note in this part of the chapter, although in those times hypnotic patterns and suggestion were used, they are not known him with these specific names in particular, but until recent time. Since these terms referred modern hypnosis. They are a recent invention. That is, they are a current linguistic creation and a modern word, used by science present as well as in other branches of medicine and therapeutics certain esoteric systems of the new era.

I'll explain a little apprentice, for we move ahead on the issue and may have a better understanding of what I'm teaching. It would not be up to mid-1700 and about 1800 AD, when the first systematic study of what became known initially as a psycho-physiological special mental state begins. Since it was only from the eighteenth century, when it began using hypnotic patterns, suggestion and persuasion openly as we know it today in modern medical science. HYPNOSIS started taking scientific and therapeutic credibility following the discovery  developed by Franz Anton Mesmer's "animal magnetism" subsequently called mesmerism later by *James Braid he is known and he popularized the term hypnosis.*

Franz Anton Mesmer was the forerunner in the eighteenth what was later known as HYPNOSIS century later. Franz Anton Mesmer was the precursor released a kind of modern hypnotism. Since this job a suggestive and persuasive systematic pattern of HYPNOSIS convinced that through the "HEALING MAGNETIC", known as the "Animal Magnetism" later called 'mesmerism' could cure many diseases. **Mesmer** Doctorate in Medicine and Philosophy at age 35 in Vienna, wrote his doctoral thesis titled PLANETARIUM INFLUXU, influenced by the theories of Paracelsus (1234-5678) on the relationship between heavenly bodies and human beings. Mesmer formulated famous Theory of Animal Magnetism we came to say that every living being radiates a type of fluidic energy like or similar physical magnetism of other bodies, and that this energy field could be transmitted from one person to another, coming to have a therapeutic application.

Mesmer, He came with a new and recent theory or how to treat diseases of people through the alleged HEALING MAGNETIC or "animal magnetism" that had to do presumably with the interrelationship between heavenly bodies and human beings, and apparently this influence helping people improve their health. His ideas and theories are not based on hypothetical assumptions unproven concepts as a real therapeutic science. But rather, thanks to their valuable contributions on the "animal magnetism" Mesmer led to the introduction of new, more precise and revolutionary ideas about what would actually be modern hypnosis today, years later.

Mesmer had the belief that among all known to science until then magnetic fields, there was an energy field which he called animated field, which was supposedly a liquid flowing in life. He defined health as the free flow of matter. That supposedly was a liquid flowing through thousands of channels throughout the human body. Mesmerize for the disease was the result of blockage of the energy flow free. The release of this lively field and the consequent restoration of this fluid in the body through hypnosis resulted in the alleged health improvement.

Mesmer had the strange belief that when nature did that free flow spontaneously in people, then they should contact a driver of course "Animal Magnetism" that Franz Anton Mesmer was a necessary and sufficient to restore the patient's health condition.

On another idea Franz Anton Mesmer believed he was a conductor of animal magnetism that assumption and that he could influence the conduct of that fluid and supposedly restore the energy field which he called animated field. Among one of the qualities of this strangely hypnotizing, Mesmer to certain movements with his hands from the patient's shoulders downward, and it was common to conduct these movements with certain magnets or magnets.

It is important to note at this point apprentice, although hypnosis is real and practical applied in ancient times different. To understand the theory proposed by mesmerism, we must understand that for the XXVIII and XIX centuries, the popular idea that time among the medical community orthodox scientific, it was that there were some invisible flows energy or influence assumptions traveling from the "hypnotherapist or hypnotist" to the patient.

For this reason, at the time of Franz Anton Mesmer HYPNOSIS of those years, he was seen by many as something in which only the hypnotist or Mesmer was solely responsible for taking the patient to those assumptions trances hypnotics; and hypnotists or hypnotists were the only ones able to bring people to these hypnotic states through the instructions and inductions allegedly owed them. Bringing as consequences the extension and creation of more taboos, myths and speculations about hypnosis. Myths, Taboos and falsities that will become clear later in detail.

To continue with the above idea apprentice, and better understand the concept of Animal Magnetism or Mesmerism as it was known then, is vitally important to understand that by the time of Franz Anton Mesmer this type of magnetic procedures or fluidic was a kind of hypnosis surrounded of theatrics and drama that had the sole purpose of keeping hypnosis as an occultist, esoteric and mystical procedure.

As I mentioned earlier, the term hypnosis as it is used and how it is known today, became popular about two centuries ago in France. The word "hypnosis" came from the Greek word "HYPNOS" which means sleep and the term "SIS" suffix meaning action, process or result of ... Therefore, hypnosis would be an action or process result of a mental state of " hyper - sugestionabilidad "also called hypnotic trance state as was defined, introduced and popularized by the already mentioned James Braid in 1843, character which is discussed in detail below.

In other words, apprentice, for this James Braid the true origin and essence of the hypnotic condition was through suggestion, induction, abstraction or mental concentration of the individual in a particular idea, which, as in a dream symbolically speaking, the powers of the human mind are absorbed to a single idea or train of thought. Creating as a result, at that time the trance state HYPNOSIS allows the individual to connect with your unconscious or subconscious mind, creating a conscious disregard of the rest of the other realities around him, and abandoned all other opinions and impressions critical thinking, thus creating new subjective reality in the subject.

<u>Practice of hypnosis in modern times</u>

As stated in the preceding paragraphs, it was around only makes about 200 to 300 years, late seventeenth and early eighteenth century, hypnosis and suggestion began to become popular and have scientific credibility and be practiced in the hands ancient and modern medical professionals, as well as other psychiatrists, neurophysiological, psychotherapists and specialists from other professional branches, they discovered that this type of therapy HYPNOTIC produced excellent subjective and mental results in improving their patients, becoming popular both in the past , as today.

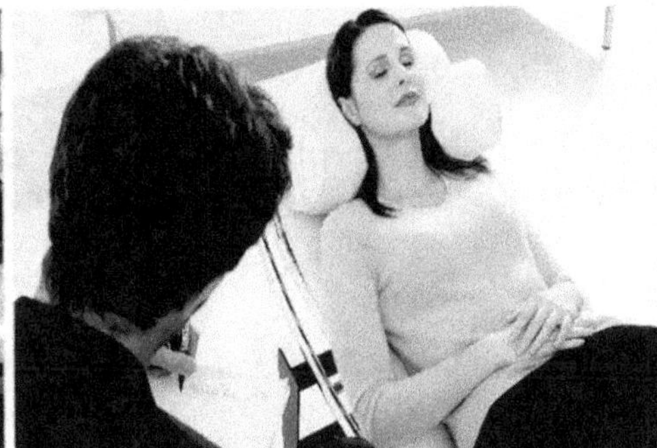

The historical analysis of the phenomena of suggestion and hypnosis, as we have been studying so far, shows his constant development and progressive evolution, with recent studies and research have produced a qualitative and quantitative changes through years. Currently no one denies that suggestion and hypnosis act on the psyche of the people; ie that can influence the strength or intensity of psychic phenomena such as perception, suggestibility, memory, thought, feelings, imagination, creativity, memories and will, among others.

Today learner day is known the close relationship between somatic and psychic aspects (Body-Mind) of human beings. It is scientifically proven that any physiological and biochemical changes in the body causes some psychic reaction and vice versa. That's why Psychosomatic and somatopsychic terms are used. And on both counts it is now possible to work with hypnosis as an effective therapy in both fields.

Of course, the use of hypnosis and suggestion as a psychotherapeutic resource has had to go through countless hardships over time, and walking paths full of obstacles and challenges in its development and historical evolution; but finally, it has been proved its medical-scientific character and significant therapeutic value in modern medicine, hypnosis becoming one of the most recognized worldwide therapies.

<u>Among the best known and famous men of history they are attributed to the pioneering studies of MODERN HYPNOSIS can mention and highlight the following historical figures:</u>

- The already aforementioned Franz Anton Mesmer (1734 - 1815), born in Germany, known as the father of modern hypnosis, was a German doctor who discovered what he called Animal Magnetism (which mainly refers to suggestion) and other follower's years later, they called Mesmerism. Franz Anton Mesmer earned his doctorate in medicine in 1766, he made his first experiments in 1773 using a technique called and became known as "HEALING MAGNETIC"; he used magnetic elements (magnets) to treat their patients. However, later it was concluded that what Mesmer did was induce or influence their patients to an altered state of mind by Persuasive Hypnotic suggestions and patterns. Mesmer made his first publication concerning the Magnetic Cure in 1775. In November 1841 Magnetizer known as LA FONTAINE, who practiced mesmerism introduced James Braid to Mesmerism and experiments, and this which popularized the term hypnosis.

• Later, the revolution and evolution of ideas and practices hypnotic Franz Anton Mesmer Animal Magnetism developer and *Mesmerism*, they made the aforementioned James Braid (1795-1860) Scottish neurosurgeon Dr., develop, define, introduce and popularize the term hypnosis and hypnotism in the scientific and medical community such as it is known today. But then the same *James Braid weather then try to rename "HYPNOSIS" by the pseudonym "MONOIDEISMO" by dimension to the theory that the proposed referring to the (fixation on one idea).* But the rapid popularization of the term and international acceptance of the name "HYPNOSIS" change prevented the pseudonym "Monoideismo" was given on subsequent dates, so that the name of the word HYPNOSIS remained unchanged until today.

James Braid caused a change in the paradigm of mesmerism eighteenth and early nineteenth century. Braid after observing demonstrations of mesmerism believed allegedly deciphered why people went to that particular state of hypnotic trance, and reaffirmed that had nothing to do with these flows assumptions magnetic forces proposed by Mesmer. Braid suggested a psychological basis for animal magnetism and concluded that the state of mesmerism (Hypnosis) was caused by fatigue of an optic nerve while maintaining stare at particular point, therefore, the association of focus vision pendulums, strobes or hypnotics discs among others, was that produced these hypnotic states.

Apparently, **James Braid** at the beginning of his theory overlooked, VERBAL suggestion that was so important in the hypnotic trance as the visual focus. Since the fact that the visual focus was what was causing the patient's eyes would feel tired and his eyelids sawed by focusing his eyes on pendulums, strobe lights or hypnotics discs, as is logical, of course. But it was the VERBAL SUGGESTION through oral INDUCTIONS what people really plunged into the desired state of hypnotic trance.

Later, in his writings, seems to shift the emphasis of his theory, though not completely abandoned the eye fixation as it said it was not just look through the visual focus, producing a hypnotic trance, but it was the VERBAL SUGGESTION through oral inductions which allowed the eye of the mind into action. In other words, when we focus on something through the visual focus and suggestion VERBAL, the conscious mind is fascinated, allowing the subconscious to focus around a single idea or train of thought, producing the expected hypnotic phenomenon.

Apprentice, to recapitulate, we can say that: James Braid defined hypnosis as "a particular state of the nervous system, that could be artificially induced by a number of strategic procedures developed for that purpose" known fastening techniques of eyes created by James Braid, ready to cause fatigue in the optic nerve through stimulation or visual approach and through verbal suggestions and inductions desired hypnotic phenomena occurred.

As we have previously read apprentice, it was between 1842 and 1843 **James Braid** popularized the term hypnotism hypnotist between the scientific and medical community, renaming MESMERISM hypnosis, with reference to the Sleep Temples Egyptians. All this after the famous publication of his book "Neuro-Psychology, or the reason for the nervous sleep considered in connection with animal magnetism, illustrated by numerous cases of successful application in relief and cure of disease" or "Neurypnology , or the rationale of Nervous Sleep Considered in relation to Animal Magnetism, Illustrated by Numerous Cases of Succesful Aplication in Relief and Cure of Disease "; where the term "hypnotism" used to refer to a state of trance or "nervous sleep" which manifested itself was normal due to the fixation and palpebral fatigue by keeping your gaze fixed on a bright object as it could be ("pendulums"), the ("strobes") or the well-known ("hypnotics discs").

As we have already mentioned previously also, the word HYPNOSIS was inspired from the Greek word "Hypnos" which means sleep and the term "Sis" suffix meaning action, process or result of ... Wanting James Braid bring as metaphorical and symbolic dimension to the HYPNOSIS as a state of numbness or deep trance-like sleep. For this reason, hypnosis today is compared metaphorically to that dream-like state of deep relaxation or state, referring to the Temples of Sleep Egyptians. But finally, we have to understand and point out that: REAL hypnosis is very different physiological sleep we know as (SLEEP) ".

For this reason, the same James Braid years after realizing that the manifestations of the hypnotic state not properly had nothing to do with the normal physiological sleep we know as the act of sleeping, tried to rename several times. His idea was to change the name of "Hypnotism" by the adjective "MONOIDEISMO" which made it more dimension to the hypothesis that he had developed the eye fixation or visual approach was (fixation on one idea). But it was so rapid popularization and acceptance of the term "hypnosis" universally prevented in successive years to achieve such a change occurs, so that the name of the term HYPNOSIS remained unchanged until today.

- *Bernheim and Liébeault:* Hippolyte Bernheim (1840-1919) French psychiatrist born in Alsace, which was added professor of the Faculty of Medicine of Strasbourg, described hypnosis as "a mental state in which a degree of hyper-suggestibility exalted occurred." This same Hippolyte Bernheim contacted a rural doctor, **Ambroise-Auguste Liébeault**, (1823-1904) founder of the School of Nancy, in the French city of Nancy 1886, dedicated to the study of hypnotic suggestion in health care. *Bernheim and Liébeault* They developed a very similar HYPNOTIC method that is used in some psychotherapeutic branches today. This methodology completely away from the turbid theatricalities and dramatizations Mesmeric method (as above). Creating a kind of therapeutic hypnosis more focused on verbal suggestions and oral inductions as part of the psychotherapeutic process without reference or reference to animal magnetism. Hippolyte Bernheim and *Ambroise-Auguste Liébeault* They created the "Psychological School of Nancy" true pioneer in the study of modern hypnosis, and opposed to the "Neurophysiological School of Paris" Hospital de la Salpetriere, founded by the most important French neurologist of the time Jean-Martin Charcot. The "Psychological School of Nancy" although little recognized in his time, had a great career and influence work in privacy by sharing publications openly, which became the predecessor teachings of modern psychosomatic medicine, and applications of hypnotic trance in such diseases (Psi - Mental).

- **Jean-Martin Charcot**, (1825-1893) One of the most influential neurologists of the time, he was a professor of pathology, head of the chair of nervous system diseases, member of the Academy of Medicine 1873 and the Academy of Sciences 1883, which together with the physician Guillaume Duchenne (1806 -1875) French clinical investigator of the nineteenth century, considered pioneers in neurology and medical photography, founded the "Neurophysiological School of Paris" pioneer of modern neurology. Both taught their lessons of neurology, psychiatry and hypnosis including being much more recognized that the "Psychological School of Nancy". One of the differences that had both schools was that the doctrine of Charcot called hypnosis as "Neurosis Experimental" stating that only could hypnotize hysterical patients, while the "Psychological School of Nancy" claimed that hypnosis could be practiced psychotherapeutically in many other cases. Contrary to the ideas of Bernheim and Liébeault, Jean-Martin Charcot postulated that hypnosis was a symptom of hysteria; and, for that reason, only those who experienced it, were those that could be hypnotizable.

- *James, Prince, Sidis:* HYPNOSIS interest remained in the United States through the writings of William James (1842-1910) American philosopher with a long and brilliant career at Harvard University, where he was professor of psychology and founder of functional psychology and great creator of literature related to hypnosis. Moreover Morton Prince (1854-1929) and contemporary American Psychiatrist psychotherapist *William James*, Was an avowed opponent of Freudianism, but brilliant supporter of hypnosis, *Morton Prince* He was one of the pioneers of the "Bostonian School of Psychotherapy" and finally Boris Sidis was another contemporary (1867-1923) Psychologist and He graduated in medicine and philosophy, was a psychiatrist who has published numerous books and articles on hypnosis, highlighting mainly in abnormal psychology, interested by the strange hypnotic manifestations of certain hysterical patients with split personality or multiple personality.

Pierre-Marie-Felix Janet (1859-1947) known simply as Pierre Janet was a French neurologist and psychologist who made important contributions to the modern study of mental and emotional disorders, and was the one who coined the concept of conscious and unconscious mind and subconscious. And he used hypnosis as a method to access the most unknown layers of consciousness. Pierre Janet originally developed the theory of dissociation and neodisociación, who argued that "decoupling" literally was the separation of some components of consciousness as a result of his work with hysterical patients. Pierre Janet HYPNOSIS believed that resulted from dissociation, and that areas of the control behavior of an individual are separated from ordinary behavior. Pierre Janet assumed that the possibility of the formation of a secondary consciousness was given by dissociation. That is, in the state of hypnotic trance formation of a second consciousness during hypnosis momentarily took the place of normal consciousness occurred. This interesting idea is also shared by many researchers today, this is ultimately a controlled state of psychic dissociation, as defined Christenson *"Hypnosis does not produce dissociation itself, but rather employs dissociation between conscious and subconscious of the subject to produce the hypnotic phenomenon 'In this case, hypnosis would remove some control from the conscious mind, allowing the individual to respond with an autonomous and reflective behavior.*

- **Josef Breuer** (1842-1925) doctor, physiologist and Austrian psychologist discoverer of ear function in regulating the balance mechanism and thermal regulation of the body by respiration. Creator of the "Method cathartic" for treating psychopathology of hysteria through hypnosis. This method was precursor analytic method of Sigmund Freud.

- Sigmund Freud (1856-1939) Austrian neurologist doctor of Jewish origin, father of psychoanalysis and one of the greatest intellectual figures of the twentieth century Hypnotic regression employed as the basis for reaching the analysis of traumatic unconscious contents. Freud later abandoned hypnotic technique to develop their own psychoanalytic method. But although Sigmund Freud was never a good hypnotist, always recognized and upheld the validity of hypnosis as an effective and therapeutic method until the end of his days.

- **Émile Coué** (1857-1926): He was a pharmacist and French psychiatrist 1857-1926. Author therapeutic method based on autosuggestion deepened in hypnosis and self-hypnosis. During the First World War this doctor, like many others suffered the lack of basic drugs to prepare your master recipes. The impotence of this fact decided nothing to tell their patients what was happening and started testing with placebos drugs, hoping to solve quickly the problem of shortages, but the normal supply of drugs prescriptions took much longer what Coué imagined. This time was the one who gave him the opportunity to observe many of his patients had done the healing process as if recovery traditionally medicated. From this observation, He began investigating the unlimited power of the human mind to heal the body and mind. His research led to these three laws called Coue laws.

- **Ivan Pávlov** (1849-1936) Russian psychologist and neurophysiologist, Nobel Prize (1904), focused his studies on higher nervous system activity on conditioned reflexes. His theories were applied in psychology, physiology, biology and of course the HYPNOSIS providing a scientific explanation. Ivan Pávlov believed that hypnosis was a partial dream. He noted that the various degrees of hypnosis did not differ perceivable and physiologically According to him, the waking state and hypnosis depended on insignificant changes of environmental stimuli. Ivan Pávlov also suggested that lower brain mechanisms were involved in hypnotic condition constant.

Moreover, Ivan Pávlov stated that the condition causing hypnosis is a monotonous and prolonged stimulation, which causes an internal inhibition is only a sleep-like stimulus response, only that propagated via a different route. According to Pavlov HYPNOSIS it limited to a sector increasingly spread reduced, leaving intact only free respiratory and cardiac centers. Another interesting contribution of its conclusions, and that helps us understand diseases, is that hypnosis is an effective psychological technique that facilitates the formation of altered states of mental awareness, which significantly delayed the organic internal processes. Hypnosis according Pávlov can be produced by various ways, orally (stories, stories, metaphors, etc. "Ericksonian Method"), eyestrain (gaze "proposed by James Braid Method"), drugs (sleeping pills "shamanic methods"), which influence the cerebral cortex inhibiting it (altering), monotonic skin touch (massage) among many back ways. In conclusion, Pávlov hypnosis is a partial sleep induced -a partial inhibition of crust- while natural sleep is total, that is, a general inhibition.

- **Dave Elman** (1900 - 1967) Important figure in the field of hypnosis and HYPNOTHERAPY. He is best known today as the author of Findings in Hypnosis (1964) and the author of an induction technique, well known and today called Dave Elman induction hypnotic. Dave Elman defines hypnosis as a mental state in which the critical faculty of the human mind is disassociated and disconnected temporarily allowing to establish a selective thinking that allows the subject to finally bring the desired state of trance. The critical faculty of your mind is that factor that goes beyond prosecution. The critical factor in mind is that part distinguishes between concepts such as hot and cold, sour and sweet, large and small or light and dark.

- **Milton H. Erickson** (1901 - 1980), born in Nevada, United States, was an American physician and hypnotherapist, innovative, and pioneer in changing TECHNICAL hypnotism applied to psychotherapy. It is recognized as the grandfather of MODERN Ericksonian Hypnosis, and is said to be the best Hypno-Therapist of all time that ever existed.

Dr. Milton H. Erickson laid the foundation for important lines within psychotherapy. NLP or NLP, Systemic Therapy Strategy, and focused therapy Solutions among other branches that were influenced by Ericksonian thought: among which the following are included psychotherapeutic approaches.

The particular origin of its characteristic and unique style of therapy can be attributed to his personal experiences as individuals, and how the same Milton H. Erickson faced his illness. And although hypnotism was an important tool in their practice, the fundamentals of its therapeutic model was the change in mental status that induced in the other person, through stories, metaphors and good relationships he had with his patients. Therapeutic model does not respond to any medical school, excluding the influence of psychoanalysis, behaviorism and systemic therapy. Milton H. Erickson is the emblematic figure of modern clinical hypnosis. Erickson created what was then called Milton Ericksonian hypnosis or method (which apprentice, is one of my specialties hypnotic).

And to achieve this, Erickson methodology used as therapy and the use of metaphors, parables, allegories, stories, tales and stories as a powerful persuasive and seductive essential tool in the hypnotic trance.

For this reason, apprentice, Dr. Milton H. Erickson thanks to its powerful influence in his time, was one of the original models, which inspired the co-creators of NLP doctors JOHN GRINDER and RICHARD BANDLER to study its methodology (Ericksonian Hypnosis) which was then incorporated as part of NLP or NLP, develop a hypnotic slope it became known later as HYPNOSIS PSYCHOLINGUISTICS.

Hypnotists, Hypnotists, hypnotists and best-known and renowned contemporary history Hypnotherapists are attributed to new studies of modern hypnosis among which we highlight are as follows:

Theodore X. Barber Oliver Zangwill, Michael Yapko, Nicolás Spanos, Harry Cannon, Ivan Jo Griffin and Tyrrell among others.

Theodore X. Barber argued that hypnotic induction techniques were naturally verbal suggestions for a particular purpose. The techniques of hypnotic induction seen from the point of view of Theodore X. Barber are a process of verbal suggestive influence that potentiates (formalizes) or deepens through a series of verbal inducements and suggestions or CULTURAL RITUALS created to achieve a previously established purpose.

On the other hand, Oliver Zangwill said in opposition to Theodore X. Barber that while cultural expectations are important in hypnotic induction, see HYPNOSIS only as a conscious process of the subjective influence on the subject, cannot alone explain hypnotic phenomena produced by these suggestions, so there must be something else. They have since recent evidence demonstrated in subjects of study in the processes of hypnotic inductions that changes in brain activity, as well as their mental and psychological processes that are directly associated experimentally hypnotic inductions declared by the hypnotist.

In turn, Michael Yapko defines hypnosis as a process of very influential effective communication, in which the hypnotist or hypnotist who guides the internal associations of the patient or participant through inductions so to establish or strengthen partnerships therapeutic through suggestions in the context of a relationship of mutual responsibility and collaborative between the therapist and the subject, whose purpose orientation between a previously established goal.

On the other hand, Nicholas Spanos hypothesized that such behaviors or conditions associated with HYPNOSIS are made with knowledge and prior approval by the patient or participant (and this of course is logical, so as it should be). Nicholas Spanos in his hypothesis claimed that there were two reasons why he explains psychologically because people involve their state of consciousness with hypnosis.

The first reason Which gives Nicholas Spanos, is suggesting that it is the same person that suggest herself with the belief that their behavior is being caused by an external source (the hypnotist) instead of themselves (of course, it is the same person that takes effect hypnotic phenomena, but under the guidance and direction of the hypnotist that through inductions redirects the subject to the desired state of hypnotic trance -. of course, we can also see the same case, sessions of self-hypnosis that this time is the same person who runs his own suggestion autohypnotic. therefore, we show here that the subject's participation is paramount to produce HYPNOSIS either induced by the hypnotherapist in a session, or are self-induced by the same person previously prepared by autohypnosis).

The second reason Nicholas Spanos proposed is related to the suggestions or inducements "cultural rituals" (termination used by Theodore X. Barber mentioned) carried out by the hypnotist. In which the hypnotist or hypnotherapist says certain subjective phrases through the suggestions and inductions, which are primarily linguistically interpreted as volunteers and later in the hypnotic procedure are now linguistically interpreted as involuntary.

FOR EXAMPLE, it happens in the next INDUCTION given by the hypnotist "Relax your leg muscles more and more" and shortly after the hypnotist utters the same suggestion as follows "The muscles in your legs are becoming more and more relaxed" (the first induction stimulates voluntary response by the subject, which helps him to begin his hypnotic process. While the second suggestion is an involuntary order by the subject, since the latter is ordered by the hypnotist to redirect the hypnotic state wanted).

It is important to note at this point that the discoveries of Nicholas Spanos had never intended to imply that the state of hypnosis does not exist. On the contrary, his studies and discovered what was intended was to show that the hypnotic behaviors exhibited by individuals under states of hypnotic trance, are due to "highly motivated and hyper-suggestible" people allowing effectively carry out either the hypnotherapeutic sessions or hypnosis show shows more effective way.

In turn, Harry Cannon defines hypnosis as a physiological mechanism by which a suggestion has a direct effect and is accepted by the subconscious of the subject through inductions. And for this to happen efficiently four things are needed:

** A focus*
** A shock*
** The suggestion itself*
** Let there be no criticism of the suggestion by the conscious intellect*

Harry Cannon when these four requirements are met, the suggestion is rooted in the subconscious and expresses itself in a leading role. This simply means that once the suggestion has been accepted by the subject is superimposed on the mind, resulting in the state of hypnosis. Harry Cannon ensures that all our learning works through hypnosis and gives the following example:

"Imagine a little boy whom his mother catches him offhandedly depriving another child what does not belong. Imagine now that, at that moment, the mother chastises her son for this action; the child in question, will now have a focus and a mind-boggling excitement about the situation. At that time, the mother wisely instructs your child to stop doing that bad action because it is wrong steals, and asks him to do it anymore. By the above criteria, this suggestion has been induced and inculcated during the formative years of the child has been stored in the subconscious without any intellectual argument by the critical factor in the mind of that little. For this experience, the child is wisely inculcated from childhood, a new social edge (programming). Whereby; Harry Cannon hypnosis is all around us, and occurs at all times and everywhere. The level of apparent intensity of hypnotic trance state is nothing more than Attestation of subjective experience of the subject and nothing else.

Jo Griffin and Tyrrell Ivan who have recently suggested a new theoretical proposition of hypnosis and mental trance. From the Human Givens Jo Griffin and Tyrrell Ivan they suggest that hypnosis is the result of having access to the REM sleep state. REM is the state that allows us to access the imagination and creativity what they call "reality generator" which is responsible for creating our dreams. One of the functions of the physiological sleep download unresolved emotional arousal during the day. In other words, the physiological sleep allows complete emotional reflections of the day through the creation of metaphorical mental images that occur as producer's links in our sleep. Its role in hypnosis is another key to update our mental model or instinctual emotional and behavioral responses. In another vein, the state of learning as well as the state of hypnosis are also a REM state. Whenever we act without conscious effort (as in the case of hypnotic trance state) it depends on certain patterns, dating back to an earlier learned response or behavior that was established in the REM state. So, when we act instinctively, in fact, we act on a post hypnotic suggestion. Similarly, when some hypnotic subject acts on a post induction or hypnotic suggestion given by the hypnotizer they will with equal effectiveness,

As we have learned so far apprentice, thanks to the contributions of Jo Griffin and Tyrrell Ivan based on its recent research on sleep, define hypnosis as any artificial means of accessing the REM state (Creative State of the Dream). Jo Griffin and Tyrrell Ivan all hypnotic phenomena, including sleepwalking, amnesia, analgesia, anesthesia, levitation of the arms, and catalepsy either eye or another member of the body, as well as hypnotic phenomena such as ideomotor responses, ideosensoriales or ideoemocionales, among other phenomena most hypnotic intensity such as regressions, distortion or disassociation of time and space, body, visual or auditory illusions, deep meditation, and for alleged mystical experiences, **Noesiology** *and even lucid dreams and astral travel, are nothing more than natural responses of the properties of the REM state, Jo Griffin and Tyrrell Ivan identified as the natural state of programming of the brain, clearly related directly by the sexual condition of cognitive aspects .*

So, when we put someone in a hypnotic trance state just as Jo Griffin and Tyrrell Ivan are activating those same processes that are activated in the brain during REM sleep state, including the "generator reality," this is what so does the effective hypnosis.

Apprentice, for your purpose as Mesmer (Hypnotist or Hypnotherapist) is useful to keep these definitions in mind when introducing a person to the state of hypnosis, as this will give you a better perspective of your work, and provide greater light to your experience and the experience of the subject.

Renaissance and Evolution of Hypnosis in current times:

From the seventies, eighties and nineties hypnosis has enjoyed a renaissance, an evolution significant recognition and positioning it as one of the most effective therapies eleventh century, emerging this time from the United States. There are a number of professionals, such as Theodore X. Barber, Oliver Zangwill, Michael Yapko, Nicolás Spanos, Harry Cannon, Jo Griffin and Tyrrell Ivan and Martin Orne, William Kroger, Herbert Spiegel, Javier Martinez Pedrós who have been responsible the significant increase in therapeutic value of hypnosis, and the use of hypnosis as a real therapy in many fields of medicine today.

This was largely due to the influence of the aforementioned Doctor MILTON H. ERICKSON. Actually, the Ericksonian approach to hypnotherapy, especially after the death of Dr. Erikson in 1980, has gained greater support. He has gained the status of alternative psychotherapy largely accepted as a medical specialty in many functional areas and professional disciplines of medicine, to be mainly a psychological mode.

Birth Ericksonian Hypnosis with Direct Clinical Methodology:

Indirect Clinical Hypnosis and Ericksonian Hypnosis appears the mid-twentieth century by the aforementioned Dr. Milton H. Erickson, which consisted of a series of metaphors, parables, allegories, stories, tales and stories as a powerful persuasive and seductive tool communication, essential in the hypnotic trance, the hypnotherapist strategically used while the patient was hypnotized.

Such metaphors, parables, allegories, stories, tales and stories should be related to the immediate problem that the patient was suffering from subtle and subjective way. A wake-up time, this kind of metaphorical language was incorporated into the psyche of the individual at a subconscious level, that allowed them to eventually help them solve their problems much more effective than traditional classical hypnosis orthodox manner.

Since such expressions, verbal, concepts and metaphorical ideas were able to subjectively stimulate a variety of sensations multisensory both at (Visual, Auditory and Kinesthetic) in subjects, which allowed them to evoke images, sounds, sensations and emotions, in the conscious and subconscious mind of the patient, producing them radically positive changes in their mental and psychological structure, creating in new neural connections more empowering, allowing participants to receive hypnotic inductions and suggestions, more useful way, holistic, comprehensive, allowing them to make new transformational ideas, thus avoiding the slightest resistance to change, and creating a greater psychological impact - emotional in the process of therapy HYPNOTIC.

The practice of this technique metaphoric language in therapy was to use the power of the spoken word in order to create confusion in the conscious mind as a suggestion it was established in the patient through indirect inductions that the subject accepted, turning them into your new reality.

The Medical-Scientific Support of hypnosis as a technique in Current Therapeutic Real

In today's time apprentice, study and research in the field of therapeutic hypnosis enjoy a good reputation. In recent decades, leading international associations of health professionals, have publicly expressed their recognition of the therapeutic usefulness of hypnosis as real and beneficial discipline, including: The American Medical Association, the British Medical Association and the American Psychological Association. This kind of international recognition, have resulted in the creation of the American Society for Clinical Hypnosis, The International Societe for Clinical and Experimental Hypnosis and the European Society of Hypnosis in Psychotherapy and Psychosomatic Medicine. Moreover, the Society of Clinical Hypnosis Therapeutics and other state-level organizations, strengthen and incorporate scientific, therapeutic, experimental and professional activity of a large number of researchers, hypnotherapists, hypnotists and hypnotists that until a few years ago, working in complete solitude, without the support of these associations. Today, there are worldwide numerous scientific institutions whose purpose is the training, development, education, implementation and disclosure, dissemination and propagation of hypnosis as a technique more in the fields of medicine, psychology, psychiatry, neurology, and the same hypnosis as a therapeutic discipline expertise. They worked in complete solitude, without the support of these associations. Today, there are worldwide numerous scientific institutions whose purpose is the training, development, education, implementation and disclosure, dissemination and propagation of hypnosis as a technique more in the fields of medicine, psychology, psychiatry, neurology, and the same hypnosis as a therapeutic discipline expertise. They worked in complete solitude, without the support of these associations. Today, there are worldwide numerous scientific institutions whose purpose is the training, development, education, implementation and disclosure, dissemination and propagation of hypnosis as a technique more in the fields of medicine, psychology, psychiatry, neurology, and the same hypnosis as a therapeutic discipline expertise.

Three important periods in the history of hypnosis:

- Time mystical, magical / esoteric, religious (Antigua Hypnosis Millenary).
- fluidic or magnetic Period (mesmerism or Hypnosis Classical Orthodox).
- evocative inductive Time (Consecration of modern scientific hypnosis).

1)At the time (mystical, magical / esoteric, religious) include shamanism, priest craft, magic, occult and religious beliefs. And of course, the Syrian mythology, Greek, Egyptian and others.

In this dark age, the strength of the influence of the power of the spoken word as a mystical, esoteric, healing and healing power was used.

And of course, the (Antigua Hypnosis Millenary) exercised his power through fear instilled through a series of rituals and full of symbols occult, songs, magic circles, candles, incense, strange sounds, among other theatrics and drama that had as sole purpose keep ANTIGUA hypnosis as a science mystical, magical / esoteric, religious, by the unfounded respect he had so much who professed hypnosis (hypnotist) as the professed religion.

2) In the second period (fluidic or magnetic with a "physical and biological" more organic perspective) At this time it was decided not by the power of the spoken word or by instilled fear, but by the belief that there was a universal energy specific called MAGNETISM. This period was characterized by the affirmation of the existence of energy fluids, where it is stated that there was an energy field they called animated field, which was supposedly a liquid flowing in life. This belief is present in medicine since its inception and founded by the Hippocratic thoughts. Their relationship, besides the Hippocratic teachings are related to the forces of the stars and has extensive links with Greek mythology.

In the fluidic or magnetic time, the ability of people to influence others and themselves transcends, as seen from the power of the spoken word to the universal energy or fluid. This search for the really efficient (energy) or (magnetism) against the speculative and theater (the human) and (verbal) making fluidic or magnetic time was a big attraction today.

Today, we can see the influence of this belief fluidic or magnetic seeing the supposed healing properties and healing that are conferred or attributed to certain minerals, bracelets, objects, pyramids and even as natural substances and everyday as the water itself, conveniently magnetized (of course, some of these elements, if they have actual proven magnetic and energetic effects on human life, while others attribute these same influences without scientifically demonstrated its validity).

At this time, it highlights the emergence of HEALING MAGNETIC "animal magnetism or mesmerism known later as was defined, introduced and popularized by the aforementioned Franz Anton Mesmer (1734-1815), recognized as a leading pioneer in the development of hypnosis modern of its kind.

3)In the third era (Hypnosis Inductive Suggestive) becomes regain the power of the spoken word as a therapeutic means, suggestive inductive (and not as able to cause fear fib). In the suggestive inductively time comprehensive, holistic and synergistic oneness between mind-body duality or no separation of mind and body proposed by **René Descartes** also seeks I dismissed (1234 - 5678). This suggestive inductively time would be the consecration of modern scientific hypnosis as we know it today, which takes into account new factors and more recent theories and scientific research CURRENT evolved from modern hypnosis.

TYPES OF HYPNOSIS "Classical and Ericksonian"

As we have seen so far apprentice, hypnosis is a real therapy constantly changing and metamorphic transformation so to speak, that has evolved through the years. Consequently, resulting in the appearance of two (2) large currents or main streams within the study and practice in the field of hypnosis in modern times are:

- ✓ **HYPNOSIS CLASSICS, FREUDIAN O SPECTACLE**
- ✓ **THERAPEUTIC HYPNOSIS ericksoniana.**

> In other words, we can say that to induce hypnosis or hypnotic trance state today, we can do it using a variety of techniques and methodologies. All of them are within one of the two currents or more famous slopes or more induction techniques known through history, which are the classical and HYPNOSIS Ericksonian hypnosis.

These two (2) types of HYPNOSIS are classic techniques, direct, authoritative, hypnosis also known as hypnosis -and- show methodologies Ericksonian therapeutic hypnosis that are more permissive or indirect cut. In which, in the latter, hypnotherapeutic techniques naturalistic, ecological and metaphoric induction suggestions are used.

Of course, that within these two (2) large groups or MAIN DIVISIONS, we can find a wide range of some very different techniques and methodologies, and some very similar between each other. Although of course, today, we can find many cases and evidence of branches and combinations between them. As in the case of psycholinguistics hypnosis or hypnosis neurolinguistics programming.

Whatever, all of them are based on conditioning ideo-sensory, ideo-motor, and ideo-emotional; stimulating the "hyper - sugestionabilidad subject through suggestion". Ie become an amplifier response or downrigger the evocative experiences of people, either to a state of hyper-concentration, hyper-creativity or hyper-relaxation as the case or particular situation in which you are using hypnosis at moment. FOR EXAMPLE: In a show Hypnosis show the "hyper - suggestibility" with hyper-creativity are favorable factors to give good entertainment. While, for example: would be more appropriate in the case of a Hypnotherapy Session hyper-concentration and hyper-relaxation.

This kind of experience commonly called "hypnotic phenomena" that occur in both cases, both show hypnosis show as the session clinical hypnosis hypnotherapeutic, what happens is that the participant or the patient experience certain personal transformations of a so much more efficient, effective and much simpler and efficient way thanks to conditioning ideo-sensory, ideo-motor, and ideo-emotional; which causes the hypnotist or hypnotherapist through the stimulation of "hyper - suggestibility" that is, that they become an amplifier response or downrigger the suggestive experiences in people, allowing you to achieve more and better results hypnotic procedures,

For this reason, this kind of hypnotic phenomena can result in the subject in question dissociation of consciousness, that is, the separation between conscious mind and subconscious, whereby the person will be able to perceive external stimuli, through attention focused on the suggestions and / or COMMANDS INDUCTIVE that they are orally transmitted by the hypnotist or hypnotherapist. Allowing respond to such stimuli or commands subjectively most effective way voluntarily ACCESSING to suggestions and inductions the hypnotist or hypnotherapist is giving, creating a new reality.

HYPNOSIS CLASSICS, FREUDIAN or Show Hypnosis

Mesmerism, the classical hypnosis, hypnosis or hypnosis Freudian show are the oldest, and consists of an enigmatic method of direct and more authoritative hypnosis. This is old school in which the hypnotist or hypnotherapist believed to have healing power to heal and improve health or suggestible and induce people to undertake certain hypnotic phenomena. This type of hypnosis, focused on the strength of the authority of the hypnotist, tone of voice, the look, gestures and body posture. Therefore, the hypnotist created around an image of mystery and power.

In this type of classical hypnosis, the hypnotist or hypnotherapist was the strong figure, therefore, gave direct orders to the patient or participant must obey. The representative of these methods was primarily the aforementioned Franz Anton Mesmer creator of animal magnetism, later called mesmerism. But it was also practiced by other great personalities like Jean-Martin Charcot and Hippolyte Bernheim, even the Sigmund Freud in its beginnings used this type of hypnosis as a therapeutic method by introducing some variants through his psychoanalytic method or hypnotic psychoanalysis, which later became known as Hypnosis Freudian.

Hypnosis Freudian, it was based on suggestion. The patient was different types of indications from the hypnotist. These inductions or suggestions can be verbal type as the well-known phrase "Go to sleep, go to sleep, go to sleep deeply," or "Sleep, Sleep, Deep Sleep" VISUALS consisting of more managerial techniques that allowed use different elements for fixing the subject's attention as it "clocks", the "strobe" and the well-known "hypnotics discs", etc. And physical techniques, consisting mainly of certain postures, gestures. This technique of the idea that, if a patient is suggested cure, or imagine a person can get hypnotic phenomenon. This method can be effective if used properly, but it is very limited, dogmatic and orthodox.

Today this kind of classical Freudian hypnosis or hypnosis is the foundation of hypnotists or hypnotists STAGE SHOW hypnotics. His techniques are more directive and authoritarian, occupying different inductive and suggestive elements for fixing the subject's attention through subliminal techniques such as visual, auditory and body mentioned above. This type of classic Freudian hypnosis or hypnosis work better than other types of hypnosis at the time of HYPNOSIS SHOW SCENARIO or hypnotics, thanks to high expectations are created in the experience, knowledge and mastery of the hypnotherapist or hypnotist. Since participants like them that "they indicate" more directly possible alternatives of hypnotic phenomena that can get to make.

> Usually costs more work to carry out, but once achieved, it takes the person deeper and deeper hypnotic trance states.

Hypnosis Classic, Freudian or Shows

The hypnotist or hypnotherapist induces in the patient or the participant to enter a hypnotic state by deepening the suggestive power of the spoken word. When it fails to produce the hypnotic trance, the suggest with the combination of an attractive scenario and statements of a large number of direct and authoritative verbal suggestive inductions that allow deepen the experience. This type of hypnosis has five (5) stages.

CLASSICAL STAGES HYPNOSIS
✓ **Induction** (relaxation).
✓ **deepening** (Account 10 to 1).
✓ **Phenomenon** Hypnotic trance or (catalepsy, analgesia, anesthesia, hallucinations, etc.)
✓ **Suggestion** posthypnotic or intervention (orders, inductions, suggestive patterns and positive direct suggestions).
✓ **Wake** (Count 1 to 19)

Apprentice, this is the oldest type of hypnotic techniques that have been employed for quite some time, both in clinical hypnosis sessions and orthodox and modern hypnotherapeutic consultation, and show street theater or hypnosis, so spectacular phenomenon. So, it has led to the idea (wrong) MYTH or taboo in which it is believed that the hypnotist dominated the mind of the person, and getting to enter hypnotic trance state to anyone with simply giving the sleeps order to sleep.

As practitioners of hypnosis techniques CLASSICAL we can mention:

- ✓ W. Kroger motivational technique. (Kroger, 1974).
- ✓ Technique fixating. (Proposed by Braid).
- ✓ Handshake technique. (By Anthony Jacquin Handshake induction)
- ✓ Method postural sway (Watkins, 1949).
- ✓ Dave Elman method (Dave Elman). Among others study us later. These techniques can be performed either with open eyes (ocular fixation), or with closed eyes, combined with (shaking hands handshake, progressive relaxation, targeted creative visualizations, etc.).

<u>Ericksonian hypnosis or Therapeutic Hypnosis</u>

Ericksonian Hypnosis or hypnosis therapy are more modern and effective. Its creator Dr. Milton H. Erickson, used it with great success and effectiveness in its hypnotic sessions, as is more permissive, that is provided to people the elements the patient or coachee needed, and this is taking voluntarily their own decisions, choices, paths and roads in the process to reach a subjective interpretation of reality that is most logical in its psychological structure or mental map. For this reason, it is one of the most powerful and functional even in light hypnotic trance states techniques.

This type of permissive methods of hypnosis, is much more effective and efficient, with lasting results in the short, medium and long-term coaching sessions and in therapeutic clinical hypnosis sessions, its main driver is the aforementioned Dr. Milton H. Erickson, who realized that the authoritarian method or orthodox classical hypnosis was not as effective in the long term, and gave no real lasting results to remain in patients.

Dr. Milton H. Erickson began using a more indirect and permissive approach, ie, instead of giving direct orders, using metaphors to convey suggestions or inductions more subjective way in the unconscious mind of the patient. If a suggestion or induction did not give results, rather than forcing the subtly modified until it was voluntarily accepted by the person.

Ericksonian hypnosis therapy was a more permissive needed voluntary and conscious participation by the patient, opposed to classical, Freudian or Shows Hypnosis was authoritative and worth of external elements to achieve that end. For example: A session of Ericksonian hypnosis could be carried out through a simple conversation (HYPNOSIS Conversational) in which the hypnotherapist leads the patient to get into a light hypnotic trance, and gradually through verbal inductions suggestive finally allowed to take the patient into a state of trance desired more intense deepening, finally allowing access gradually to the unconscious mind and subconscious mind of the patient, free and subtly.

Ericksonian Hypnosis or therapeutic hypnosis consist of lead patients to a state of trance, but without the direct and authoritative suggestion posed by the Hypnosis Classic, Freudian or Shows. The latter is more participatory and dialogue with the person who receives it, with the methodology the metaphorical language used by the hypnotherapist, it becomes more symbolic.

In other words, we can say that Ericksonian hypnosis more emphasis on the ability of the patient to voluntarily participate in the hypnotic sessions, regardless of both the unconscious state of trance (hypnotic phenomenon) as the intentional predisposition of the patient to perform the therapy.

This type of methodology used as therapeutic hypnosis, using metaphors, parabolas, allegories, stories, tales and stories through conversational hypnosis in conjunction with certain HYPNOTICS PATTERNS persuasive used as a powerful tool influential and seductive essential in HYPNOTIC TRANCE. Making all these elements synergistically an effective tool to achieve the desired hypnotic state. It has been shown that this type of Ericksonian hypnotherapy is very effective in many cases, for example: Stop drinking, smoking or lose weight with hypnosis.

It is for this reason that hypnosis Ericksonian or Therapeutic Hypnosis is widely used by most modern hypnotherapists today. One of the qualities of hypnotherapy developed by Dr. Milton H. Erickson, is that belies created taboos or myths about hypnosis as are: The belief of having to "deep sleep" let go and "get lost in the unconscious "and" subject yourself to the will of the hypnotist "to bring about a change in habits of behavior or way of perceiving problems, since as we have seen in previous sections, this is not real, and it is absolutely false for several reasons.

1 The trance state is not sleep, this is only metaphorical, since we need to keep awake to receive the suggestions of the hypnotist.
2nd In the state of trance we always remain aware of our actions, so in no time we get lost in the unconscious.
3rd The participant or patient never subject to the will of the hypnotherapist, only allows voluntarily receive suggestions, which eventually allow the desired changes, if the person so wishes.

Ericksonian Hypnosis or Therapeutic Hypnosis is more linked to our current way of life, and is generally more accepted by patients, coachees and people in general, for the seriousness and ethical accounting, as this new school of hypnosis is much more respectful of the principles and values of the patient, and is much more effective than the predecessor, because nowadays, people avoid the "theatrics" unfounded fears that originated in the past.

Ericksonian hypnosis or Therapeutic Hypnosis

As we have mentioned above, Ericksonian Hypnosis or Therapeutic Hypnosis, or the degree of suggestibility and depth of the hypnotic trance is more important, but rather, it focuses primarily on the ability of the patient to voluntarily participate in the hypnotic sessions, not importing both the unconscious state of trance (hypnotic phenomenon) and intentional and voluntary willingness of the person who is performing the therapy.

Even with the "CONVERSATIONAL HYPNOSIS" or "PATTERNS HYPNOTICS Persuasive" extraordinary results are achieved in people, subtle and subjectively without entering the person into a state of deep hypnotic trance. Since the key is the verbal language used.

That is, the key to this type of Ericksonian hypnosis or THERAPEUTIC HYPNOSIS is based on effective communication, through suggestive hypnotic patterns and commands that are communicated to the patient or participant through metaphoric and symbolic language. Since this type of verbal expressions, suggestions and subtle inductions are able to subjectively stimulate a variety of multi-sensory both level (visual, auditory and kinesthetic) in the patient or participant feelings, which bring to mind images, sounds, sensations and emotions in the mind of the subject, which eventually allow them to adopt new ideas, thus avoiding the slightest resistance to change, and creating a greater psychological impact - emotional in the process of hypnotic suggestibility autosuggestion or hyper-conscious.

Such HYPNOSIS is characterized by the following elements:

✓ Sharpen the patient to the positive and desired end result.
✓ Provide indirect suggestions, not authoritarian or tax.
✓ Using figurative language and metaphors to induce permanent results.
✓ Direct therapy to finding an agreed with the patient and the hypnotherapist previously from the first session solution.
✓ Power domestic remedies that the patient already has so you can fix problems alone or to enhance learning.
✓ Respect the principles and intrinsic values of the patient, allowing them to go through a gradual process of positive change, without imposing direct orders, but suggestions through subtle suggestions and hypnotic inductions effective according to the needs of each person.

<u>Psycholinguistics hypnosis or NLP hypnosis</u>

Psycholinguistics Hypnosis or hypnosis neurolinguistics programming (NLP) is a model of effective interpersonal communication that is primarily concerned with the relationship between behavior and the subjective experiences of people through hypnosis. In particular, models underlying thinking stimulated by hypnotic phenomena.

hypnosis Psycholinguistics hypnosis or Neuro Linguistic Programming is also an alternative hypnotherapy system that aims to educate people on a self-discovery of consciousness through hypnosis and effective communication. And thus, it aims to change their patterns of mental and emotional behavior through the metamodel.

HYPNOSIS PSYCHOLINGUISTICS or hypnosis neurolinguistics programming is a technique of recent HYPNOSIS very interesting, evolving that takes the best of HYPNOSIS classic and Ericksonian Hypnosis and merges with the Family Therapy and Psychotherapy Gestalt, but adds a very special component metamodel of language that is the precursor of the theory of transformational grammar of Chomsky in relation to the Surface Structure and Deep Structure (1956-1966).

Doctors studies JOHN GRINDER (Psychologist, Linguist) and RICHARD BANDLER (*mathematician, gestalt psychologist and computer expert)* clearly show that what distinguishes us especially other living beings is precisely language. Even our thoughts are "impregnated" or "registered" in relation to the language we use and meaning, in short, much of our behavior is determined by the language we use, with which we were raised and with which we express ourselves.

In psycholinguistics hypnosis or hypnosis neurolinguistics programming, the term "Superficial Structure" is used to refer to the language and sensory experiences through a set of words and sounds (for speech), or symbols, signs and images, (for the writing). From inside the deep structure to the externalization message in the surface structure, the context or content of experience is transformed as it approaches the surface. Importantly, both the language and the sensory experience of the patient or coachee belong to different logic levels, and each representational mode can be translated by the language spoken or written either by words or phrases. In other words,

Moreover, apprentice, in hypnosis PSYCHOLINGUISTICS or hypnosis neurolinguistics programming, the term "Deep Structure" is used to refer to the meaning of each word and sounds (speech), or symbols, signs and images (in the written) for each person according to their inner experience. The deep structure represents - Mind - supporting or containing the meaning of the sentence. (It's abstract). So, the PNL or NLP considers the deep structure is composed of sensory and emotional experiences. And consider the spoken or written as a secondary experience derived through primary language experiences. To take this into account in the hypnosis sessions, it is much easier to provoke in the subject a dissociation of consciousness, is the separation between Conscious mind and SUBCONSCIOUS using the metamodel LANGUAGE, to achieve this end. In order that the person is able to perceive external stimuli, through attention focused on the suggestions and / or inductive orders they were being transmitted orally, allowing react or respond to such stimuli Subjectively, voluntarily accessing suggestions and inductions the hypnotist is giving you.

LANGUAGE metamodel was developed by Grinder and Bandler doctors as a means to work with the surface structure of language to help people enrich their world model regaining its deep structure and reconnecting with primary experience. Since somehow, all techniques HYPNOSIS NLP are an attempt to create greater and better overall holistic connection between the surface structure and the deep structure of the patient or coachee. Allowing use these models to change the way in which subject's record events in their mental structure.

In another vein, we can say that hypnosis PSYCHOLINGUISTICS or hypnosis neurolinguistics programming are linguistic interventions that make the patient or coachee improve modifying internal programs of action using Metamodel LANGUAGE, why Ericksonian Hypnosis has a lot relationship with NLP Hypnosis.

<u>WHAT IS A metamodel? and How Hypnosis applies to?</u>

The metamodel is the study of language structure and meaning; and how it affects each person subjectively. From the viewpoint of NLP, META derived from Greek and means INSIDE "or" beyond. A metamodel is then within a representation or model that goes beyond representation models. Therefore, the meta-language model would be a set of perfect form or hypnotic suggestions that goes into a series of "key questions" or questions intelligent inductive, suggestions and inductions that go beyond words, to improve our processes communication in the states of hypnotic trance.

For this reason, the Model Magic Questions through the suggestions and inductions proposed by the HYPNOSIS PSYCHOLINGUISTICS hypnosis or NLP is known by the term metamodel HYPNOTIC LANGUAGE.

As we have learned so far, and there is a wide variety of hypnotic techniques. The method chosen depends on what you want to achieve, as well as personal preferences of each person participating in the hypnosis sessions. It is important to note at this point, the hypnotist, hypnotist or hypnotherapist will choose and recommend the best technique according to the need of the subject.

For example, one of the most effective methods that can be used in a hypnotherapy in a coaching session, or NLP hypnosis session would Ericksonian Hypnosis. Since this allows the hypnotherapist take the hypnosis session, using the metaphoric and symbolic language, speaking in a tone of gentle, unhurried and relaxed voice, describing images that create in the patient or coachee a feeling of relaxation, deepening, security and wellness. While the subject in question is under the hypnotic trance, the hypnotherapist suggests appropriate ways in which the patient can achieve specific goals through subjective and indirect inductions that allow them to achieve some particular purpose suggestions. These suggestions and inductions could be used as appropriate for each particular person, for example,

How can appreciate apprentice odds with this type of Therapeutic Hypnosis Ericksonian are endless, of course, they are subject to the ability to "hyper - suggestibility" of the person accessing the hypnotic trance and the ability of the hypnotherapist to amplify the answers to suggestive through deepening experiences of people which is hypnotizing and achieve the desired objectives.

Another very effective technique in this case applied to both the HYPNOSIS PSYCHOLINGUISTICS as hypnosis CLASSIC is self-visualization, which allows the hypnotherapist or hypnotist once led to enter a state of deep the subject hypnotic trance, through techniques hypnosis helps the participant to stimulate their "hyper - suggestibility" to activate your "hyper - imagination" or "hyper - creativity" to accept orders both direct and indirect through suggestions and specific inductions that create certain mental images entitling the subject clearly visualize and play the hypnotic phenomenon is to be achieved.

This visual creating mental images or vivid pictures of a specific situation are known as mental visualizations, and is one of the suggestive techniques and inductive both HYPNOSIS PSYCHOLINGUISTICS and the HYPNOSIS CLASSICS, because it is very powerful to help participants or patients to achieve the desired to be achieved hypnotic phenomenon. For example, it makes the person a situation of immobility either eye, arms or other limbs of your body, this action is known in the world of hypnosis as catalepsy imagine. Once suggest the subject with direct and indirect to create and reproduce such immobility or catalepsy in any part of your body specific inductions, deepening hypnotic experience begins through verbal orders and suggestions, subjective and direct and indirect continuous and progressive inductions suggestions, ranging causing the participant finally immobility or catalepsy, once entered into the hypnotic trance and accepted the suggestions of the hypnotist and suggestive inductions the hypnotist ordering it subtly lose mobility that momentary body which imagined and ordered to freeze. Having achieved this first goal, the hypnotist proceeds through deepening strengthen the reality created in the subconscious mind of the subject through verbal suggestions.

A third very powerful technique; in this case hypnotherapy is self-hypnosis. Hypnotist or hypnotherapist where teaches the individual to induce a state of hypnosis itself. And then the person; you can continue using this skill on their own, once he learned the technique and methodology to help also overcome certain habits or improve their self-confidence and personal safety, whenever they need it. Importantly, all hypnosis is self-hypnosis and relaxation are all self-relaxation. Since the hypnotist gives a number of suggestions and instructions, but is the subject matter which repeats itself, auto suggesting and arriving at desired hypnotic state. In other words, all kinds of Ericksonian hypnosis is this,

"Success is not a one-day event, it is a lifelong process is repeated. You can be a winner in his life if he tries. BECAUSE YOU ARE A WINNER born and from the moment of conception ... Remember: Successful people engage in activities that allow them to win from time to time; because they know that both the triumph, victory and conquest are habits that should constantly develop in their lifestyle ... Successful people; Also, they keep in mind that it is also losing wins. Because they know that every failure brings them closer to their purpose and that every defeat strengthens and teaches them what to improve. In After; both triumphs and defeats, are so important for success, that when we learn from them we become stronger and worthy of living that style and extraordinary quality of life for which we have both strive day after day. "- YLICH TARAZONA. -

Good **LEARNERS, we have reached the end of this lesson, here you have learned about HYPNOSIS history of its evolution and development through the centuries!** I HOPE YOU HAVE LIKED this first introductory chapter ... If you have any questions or if something just did not understand; quiet is normal, when you start a new learning :). Good; keep in mind that, *"If you have any questions, you can "write directly to me (E-mail).*

MásterCoach.YlichTarazona@gmail.com
http://www.reingenieriamentalconpnl.com

THE POWER OF PURPOSE: *"Knowing what the purpose that gives meaning to our existence, is what ultimately allows us to rediscover why we are here and we are born. Let us remember that we are all born with a purpose, all have a mission. And when we discover and we pursue it, this will not only give meaning to our existence, but open endless chances to take us straight to our destination. "- YLICH TARAZONA. -*

CHAPTER II: DEFINITIONS, CONCEPTS, THEORIES AND PRINCIPLES BASIC HYPNOSIS

Hello such, champions and champions, I'm glad we already find in the second chapter of this book, in Part I introduced you in the history of hypnosis its evolution and development over the centuries. Now apprentice studying enter Definitions, concepts, theories and basic principles of hypnosis. - To begin this second chapter is conducive knows the **Definition of the word hypno-SIS by its origin in the Greek root:**

• "Hypno" That means "dream" comes from Greek mythology (Hypnos), which was the personification of (sleep), son of Erebus (god of darkness and shadow) and Nix (goddess of night) and twin brother of Thanatos (death god) and father of Morfeo (god of sleep).

• "SIS": Suffix meaning action, process, result ... or irregular state of mind. Therefore, hypnosis would be an action or process result of an irregular state of mind - synergistically combined and merged with states of "hyper - imagination," "hyper suggestibility", "hyper - creativity" and "hyper - concentration" Creating as result, the individual will connect to your unconscious or subconscious mind, creating a conscious disregard of the rest of the other realities or perceptions around, he abandoned all other ideas, opinions and impressions of thought, creating a new subjective reality.

For this reason, apprentice, hypno-SIS to come from the Greek word (Hypnos) which means sleep is associated symbolically and metaphorically to numbness, sleep or lethargy but remember that the term hypnosis is only an allegorical reference GREEK MYTHOLOGY (Hypnos) and EGYPTIAN ANCIENT PRACTICES that are associated with (Sleep Temples Egyptians) practiced in ancient times. Although at present and in actual practice, modern hypnosis has nothing to do with the act of "falling asleep or doze SOUND" literally.

As it has been scientifically proven hypnosis is "A normal physiological state of man where certain similar to REM sleep physiological phenomena, which, when activated by the suggestions and hypnotic inductions declared by the hypnotist, allows the appearance of responses occur ideo motor, sensory ideo, and ideo-emotional, but the subject in question always remains awake and alert at all times, just in a state of relaxation and much higher than the waking state concentration.

While it is true that certain features of REM sleep state come into play in the hypnotic process; Apprentice is important to note, as we have already clarified earlier that the state of hypnotic trance is very different to normal physiological sleep we know as the act of (SLEEP) ". Since I repeat, at any time during the procedure, people in the state of hypnotic trance fall into something like a deep sleep, much less literally sleep in the trance.

Definitions HYPNOSIS

Hypnosis is a state of mind or a group of attitudes generated through a discipline called hypnotism. Usually, hypnosis consists of a series of verbal instructions and preliminary suggestions. Such inductions can be generated by a hypnotist, hypnotist or hypnotherapist in therapy or hypnosis session as well as can be "self-induced (autosuggestion)" by the same person "self-hypnosis".

When using hypnosis, one person (the subject "participant or patient") is directed or guided by a specialist (the hypnotist, hypnotist or hypnotist) to respond to verbal suggestions and preliminary inductions in exchange for subjective inner experiences. These subjective inner experiences or hypnotic phenomena occurring in (the subject "participant or patient") alter your perception of reality, like an amplification of multisensory sensations that increase the levels of hyper-suggestibility stimulating and redirecting their emotions, thoughts, emotions, actions and behavior to a desired hypnotic state. In other words, Hypnosis is a state of mind amplifier internal responses or downrigger of the evocative experiences that are experiencing (the subject "participant or patient") through an induced hypnotic state that allows the appearance of answers ideo motor, sensory ideo, and ideo which empowers the-emotional person achieve more and better results with hypnotic procedures. Of course, apprentice, who in this discipline people can also learn to "self-induced or (auto-suggestible)" and themselves through self-hypnosis, which is the capacity or ability to use effective self-hypnotic procedures in oneself and generating positive and favorable changes you want. ideo sensory, emotional and ideological that empowers people to achieve more and better results with hypnotic procedures. Of course, apprentice, who in this discipline people can also learn to "self-induced or (auto-suggestible)" and themselves through self-hypnosis, which is the capacity or ability to use effective self-hypnotic procedures in oneself and generating positive and favorable changes you want. ideo sensory, emotional and ideological that empowers people to achieve more and better results with hypnotic procedures. Of course, apprentice, who in this discipline people can also learn to "self-induced or (auto-suggestible)" and themselves through self-hypnosis, which is the capacity or ability to use effective self-hypnotic procedures in oneself and generating positive and favorable changes you want.

For these reasons, we can reaffirm that hypnosis temporarily causes the subject a dissociation of consciousness, ie, the temporary separation of critical factor between your mind conscious and the unconscious or subconscious mind, thus, people are able to perceive and experience external stimuli, through attention focused on the suggestions and / or inductive orders were being transmitted through specialist (hypnotist, hypnotist or Mesmer), allowing thus respond positively and affirmatively to such stimuli or orders subjectively most effective way, agreeing voluntarily to the suggestions and inductions received, thus creating this new reality.

It is important to note that the use of hypnosis for therapeutic purposes is known as HYPNOTHERAPY. Although hypnosis is also used for entertainment purposes, as is in the case of shows hypnosis shows.

OTHER DEFINITION AND THEORIES KNOWN OF HYPNOSIS LESS:

Theory of State and Theta Alpha. Thanks to the data collected by the electro-encephalography, the four major schemes frequency levels or brain waves of electrical impulses that trigger the brain have been identified. This theory teaches that hypnosis or trance states HYPNOTIC are nothing more than a temporary transformation of consciousness of hyper suggestibility at the moment mindfulness of the individual decreases in their levels of frequencies and brainwave ALFA / ALPHA 13 to 8Hz or cycles per second "TRANCE LIGHTWEIGHT" or between 7-4 Hz or cycles per second levels and brain wave frequencies ZETA / THETA "DEEP hypnosis." Allowing move from the perception of the outside world, to the perception that exists within ourselves.

FOR EXAMPLE: It happens in the case of the ancient sessions of Tibetan monks entering a kind of meditative state DEEP, allowing them to activate their Pineal gland and therefore conscious powers of what they call higher consciousness that allows them to activate a type of lucid dreaming or astral projection through meditation, due to a narrow attentional focus to a single particular idea or state of higher consciousness, which they call enlightened state.

Another physiological definition attributed to the theory of State ALPHA AND THETA HYPNOSIS is corroborating that the level and frequency brain waves of electrical impulses needed and more conducive to work on issues such as changes in behavior, conduct, paradigms, habits, moods, feelings, emotions and thoughts, is the state ALFA / ALPHA. ALFA / ALPHA state is also conducive to stimulating the capacities of the conscious mind and activate the unlimited powers of the subconscious mind. Another physiological statement attributed to HYPNOSIS theory STATE AND ALPHA THETA is claiming that the State ZETA / THETA is required for a therapeutic change of greater significance. The ZETA / THETA STATE is also associated for example with SURGICAL HYPNOSIS,

Another of the most recent discoveries and greater significance in the study of hypnosis as it has been shown through the years, and has been demonstrated in hundreds of studies and research on the theory of State ALPHA AND THETA, is that HYPNOSIS or HYPNOTIC STATE OF TRANCE really is a meditative and intuitive faculty developed most individuals without realizing it.

> ***FOR EXAMPLE****: The vast majority of people in some way or another entered and permanently out of "states of hypnotic trances" "states ALFA / ALPHA" or "altered state of consciousness" as it is called. A good example of this statement would be, to give an everyday example; when we walked in, caught up in an idea, thought or event, distracted lift after a few seconds the door opens, and without our accounts we got off the elevator, and then realize that we are still missing some other floors to do so.*
>
> ***Another good example*** *Very common in the states of hypnotic trance involuntary often happens when we drive our car, and we know exactly where we have to cross to get to our destination, but for a while we get distracted in an idea, thought or event, then in matters of seconds, we enter a "ALFA / ALPHA state" or "altered state of consciousness" which makes the crossing we had because we were distracted thinking about something else. APPRENTICE This means that a lesser or greater degree, everyone went into "trances HYPNOTICS" INVOLUNTARY or "altered state of consciousness" unconsciously.*

As we could give us how much apprentice; by the above examples, people not only come again and again in trances HYPNOTIC UNCONSCIOUS, but also have the power to put into trance to others. And I'm going to show.

*****A good example of this****: It happens when we tell someone a fascinating story, or you recount an event or situation which we live, and do it with such intensity and emotion that the listener we begin to be able to vividly imagine the situation, and recreate in their mind every event as if he were living person at that moment. "{[At this time, the person who listens attentively history, is so absorbed in the story, which goes into a state of trance ALFA or" altered states of consciousness "without even realizing it or notice]}".*

And this same apprentice situation of "altered state of consciousness" happens and repeats very regularly, for example: When we see a good movie and we move both the stories and the argument itself, the film ends by immersing ourselves in frame, so that the film were HYPNOTIZED. In such a way that finally begin to recreate the same situations, events, experiences, thoughts, feelings and emotional states through which the protagonists are going through. To this point; so, we experience their same emotions, whether those of fear, horror, suspense, drama, pain, sadness, joy, happiness, love, passion, excitement, sensuality and even desire. Anyway, we generate a lot of multisensory situations that cause us an unconscious response in our bodies and we call HYPNOTIC TRANCE STATE OF INVOLUNTARY. And all these multisensory stimuli apprentice happen within us internally, without even noticing them. That is, that all these unconscious responses happen in our subconscious mind through these sensory representations (visual, auditory or kinesthetic) which we live and experience in our daily lives daily every day.

Brainwaves and EEG frequencies or statements and activity related to Hypnosis Neuronal oscillatory.

To continue the previous issue of THEORY OF STATE ALPHA AND THETA and frequency levels or brain waves, we could reaffirm medically speaking the "STATE OF TRANCE HYPNOTIC" we recognize by a decrease in neuronal activity and decreasing levels of brainwave frequencies or neuronal oscillatory activity.

FOR EXAMPLE: If we connect an EEG or (Electroencephalogram) in the head of an individual, it will indicate a neural frequency or frequencies greater BETA brainwaves to 14 Hz or cycles per second, when in the waking state (ie the normal state maximum alert).

Between 13-8 Hz or cycles per second brainwave ALPHA / ALPHA when we enter a trance Light (For example, states of relaxation, concentration, meditation, hyper-suggestion, as well as the states of involuntary hypnotic trance known as "unconscious distraction" latter learner related shared above examples).

Between 7 and 4 Hz or cycles per second brainwave ZETA / THETA passing to TRANCE DEEP (For example, in trances where hypnotic phenomena occurring within the HYPNOSIS as well as are the states of relaxation, concentration and deep meditation achieved through certain disciplines as Tibetan Buddhism). In this state ZETA / THETA are also people who have sleep empowers experience lucid, body experiences or astral travel).

Between 3 and 2 Hz or cycles per second brainwave DELTA means the state where we (asleep or faint) "These two last 2 has nothing to do with hypnosis" If mark 1 to 0.5 cycles mean that are in a (coma) and finally the 0 indicates (death).

Based on these scales and studies closely related to levels of frequencies and brain waves, we can say clearly that the vast majority of people, we have entered in some way or another in the ALFA / ALPHA states of light hypnotic trance (from 13 to 8 Hz or cycles per second of brain) waves unconscious and involuntarily.

What happens in these cases is that we do not realize it because we had no reference to serve us to distinguish a "state of consciousness altered oriented internal processes," which would allow us to distinguish a "ALFA / ALPHA state process-oriented external perception. "

To sum up, we can say that the hypnotic trance is thus a very effective method used systematically (we are aware of it or not) to transfer a person from one state of consciousness to another (whether this process consciously or unconsciously).

Wherein said person entering the hypnotic trance or state of "hyper-suggestibility" or "hyper-creativity" is an amplifier response or downrigger the suggestive experiences or state "hyper concentration" and relaxation allowing you to experience personal transformations of a much more effective way, effective and simpler way, if perform the same procedure in the State ALERT or wakeful state.

BRIEF OUTLINE brainwaves and EEG FREQUENCY OR NEURONAL oscillatory activity states.

WAVES BETA = Between 14 to 28 Hz or (cycles per second or cps)
STATE OF MONITORS, fully awake, alert and active with the 5 senses.
State concentration conducive to focus on a specific activity.

WAVES ALPHA / ALPHA = 8 to 13 Hz or (cycles per second or cps)
Trancelike state LIGHTWEIGHT
State of meditation, relaxation and concentration
State conducive to start making practice self-hypnosis and hypnosis.
State conducive to remember dreams and induce lucid dreams cause.
Relaxed state conducive to activate creativity or creative thinking and improve the teaching process - learning.

WAVES ZETA / THETA = 4 to 7 Hz or (cycles per second or cps)
Sleepiness state or dream state and deep relaxation.
ONIRICAL state or state TWILIGHT conducive to stimulate and create lucid dreams, astral travel or cause Extra Body Experiences.

WAVES DELTA = 0,5 3 Hz or (cycles per second or cps)

State of sleep, relaxation, meditation or deep trance

State conducive to creating hypnotic phenomena high level, and stimulate hyper - sugestionabilidad, hyper-creativity and hyper-concentration at higher levels **allowing the emergence of ideo motor responses, sensory ideo, and ideo-emotional.** *That is, the state* **DELTA** *an amplifier or downrigger response suggestive of experiences and* **extra sensory**, *physical and mental.*

WAVES GAMMA = High to above 40 Hz (cycles per second or cps)

The latter Brainwave or oscillatory Neuronal Activity States is the most recently discovered on the updates frequently. So, they say; It related the latest and most recent studies on the subject of EEG frequencies and THEORY OF STATE AND ALPHA THETA.

State or level of introspection

State insight, knowledge and flurry of high-level information processing and explosive bursts of creative ideas.

These brain waves or oscillatory Neuronal Activity States GAMMA are popularly known as EUREKA STATE.

GRADES, LEVELS AND HYPNOTIC TRANCE STATES BY THE SCALE OF ERIC BARONE

STATE OF MONITORS "Z0" - present here and now.

Conscious state characterized by high frequency or brain waves in neuronal activity STATE = BETA Between 14 to 28 Hz or (cycles per second or cps)

It is the open expression of feelings and sensory perceptions (VAK "O and G") Visual, auditory and sensory "Kinesthetic".

Receive and accept simple suggestions, positive affirmations, inductions and patterns through a circle conversational hypnosis power or force level Authority Level "FP0" and "FP1".

State concentration conducive to focus on a specific activity, is characterized by the expression of verbal and non-verbal language, memory, emotions, memories, instincts, attention, desires and knowledge.

It is characterized by staying fully awake, alert and active with the 5 senses (sight, hearing, touch, taste and smell).

STATE HIPNOIDAL or Incantation Z0 and Z1.

Semi-conscious state, characterized by decreasing the frequency levels or brain waves in neuronal activity STATE ALPHA / ALPHA = 8 to 13 Hz or (cycles per second or cps)

LIGHTWEIGHT trancelike state conducive to start performing self-hypnosis, hypnosis practice and is a favorable state to receive and accept simple suggestions, positive affirmations, progressive inductions and hypnotic patterns basic circle power or force level Authority Level "FP1" and "FP2".

In this state, the subject is aware of everything that happens in their environment, so sometimes could doubt his hipnoidal hypnotic trance state. Mostly waking time will evaluate incorrectly believe that it's been ten minutes when in fact it's been a much longer time.

It makes us more suggestible to emotions and feelings.

hypnotic state that occurs naturally or created, for example:

- ✓ Seeing a movie, going to the movies, listen to certain music.
- ✓ While we recite a prayer or a mantra.
- ✓ While we dive into reading a good book.
- ✓ When we are in love - infatuation or enchantment.
- ✓ When we have a slight loss of sense of time.
- ✓ When we receptiveness to certain advertising or publicity.
- ✓ It manifests when we daydream or visualize.
- ✓ While a class or witness heard a talk or conference.

It is characterized by the following HYPNOTICS PHENOMENA

- ✓ Mental relaxation
- ✓ Physical relaxation
- ✓ Partial decreased breathing
- ✓ Partial decreased pulse or heartbeat
- ✓ Feeling mild lethargy
- ✓ Feeling faint CATALEPSY
- ✓ Partial closure of eyes
- ✓ Increased number of flutter
- ✓ Partial sluggishness of mind
- ✓ The person becomes more susceptible to suggestions and inductions of a circle power level Force or Authority Level "FP1" and "FP2".

Superficial HYPNOTIC TRANCE MILD or Z1.

Semi-conscious state, characterized by a further decrease of the frequency levels or brain waves in neuronal activity STATE ZETA / THETA = 4 to 7 Hz or (cycles per second or cps)

It is conducive to accept and receive a larger amount and direct suggestions and mild suggestive inductions and hypnotic patterns and commands a circle progressive power level Force or Authority Level "FP3" and "FP4".

In this state, the subject is aware of everything happening around him, so sometimes could doubt under the influence of mild hypnotic state, but upon awakening evaluate the time has elapsed without realizing it at all, will believe It is having spent time when it actually happened much more than perceived.

State conducive to practice relaxation, meditation, concentration and developing states excellence through hypnosis.

State practice conducive to intimacy and sexual relations to a higher level multiorgasmic type Tibetan tantric sex or Hindu sex "Kama Sutra".

ONIRICAL state or state *TWILIGHT* conducive to stimulate and create lucid dreams, astral travel or lead-body experiences.

State conducive to start influence and induce positive changes in our thoughts, feelings, behaviors and habits.

It is characterized by the following HYPNOTICS PHENOMENA

✓ Greater control of emotions and feelings
✓ Decreased breathing, this slows
✓ gradual decrease of the pulse or heart rate
✓ Feeling of lethargy or mental and physical sluggishness
✓ Ocular sensation catalepsy and tips
✓ Close your eyes and increase the number of flutter
✓ Increased empathy, allowing create greater rapport in hypnosis sessions or show of shows
✓ The person becomes more susceptible to suggestions and inductions being more conducive to receiving and accepting direct orders
✓ State conducive to practicing hypnosis sessions, coaching and NLP among other alternative practices such as reiki, yoga, tai chi or acupuncture.
✓ Increased capacity Reflex (Martial Arts)
✓ Been supportive and very effective to program the mind to brain reengineering, practice hypnopedia, Self-hypnosis, auto-suggestion, self-display or learn or practice some new language or skill.
✓ The person becomes more susceptible to suggestions and inductions of a circle power level Force or Authority Level "FP3" and "FP4".

HYPNOTIC TRANCE MEDIUM or cataleptic Z1 and Z2.

State of semi-major unconsciousness, characterized by a further decrease of the frequency levels or brain waves in the neuronal activity externally perceptible STATE ZETA / THETA = 4 to 7 Hz or (cycles per second)

It is suitable to receive and accept a greater number of suggestions, inductions and direct through hypnotic patterns circle power level Force or Authority Level "FP5" and "FP6" subjective orders.

It is characterized by the following HYPNOTICS PHENOMENA

✓ Hypnotic phenomenon Anesthesia and Analgesia Low and Medium (tolerance and capacity susceptible to relieve and control certain degree of pain) Effect Fakir - carried over needle, local surgical anesthesia.
✓ Amnesia light and medium, ability to forget certain ideas or simple, such as names, dates, numbers, colors, smells, tastes and events.
✓ Hypnotic phenomenon Lethargy, Catalepsy and cataleptic Middle Catatonic
✓ Ability to maintain Hypnotic Trance Medium or cataleptic, either with eyes open or closed.
✓ This status Hypnotic or cataleptic Middle It allows the subject to accept an inhibition (A slight ban) start leaving such a bad habit.
✓ *Accepts and receives direct suggestions, commands, patterns and hypnotic inductions average intensity of a circle power level Force or Authority Level* "FP5" and "FP6".
✓ ONIRICAL state or state *TWILIGHT* conducive to stimulate, create maintain lucid dreams, astral travel and extra cause bodily experiences.
✓ Levels multi-sensory hallucinations visual, auditory and kinesthetic, olfactory and gustatory
✓ Ability to enter and maintain deep levels of relaxation, meditation, concentration and Hiper Suggestibility.

HYPNOTIC TRANCE THRESHOLD somnambulistic or somnambulistic Z2.

Hypnotic trance state Mayor, which is characterized by a higher degree of decreasing frequency levels or brain waves in neuronal activity STATE DELTA = 0,5 3 Hz or (cycles per second or cps), externally perceivable.

✓ It is suitable to receive and accept a greater number of suggestions, inductions and subjective through hypnotic patterns and commands a circle power level Force or Authority Level "FP7" and "FP8" direct orders.

✓ This status hypnotic somnambulistic It allows the subject to accept inhibitions (A mid- and high-ban) stop or control such a bad habit.

State conducive to the practice of Sessions and Show, Regressions and trances.

It is characterized by the following HYPNOTICS PHENOMENA

✓ *State conducive to creating hypnotic phenomena and stimulate "Hyper - suggestibility"" Hyper-creativity "and" hyper-concentration "* **allowing the emergence of ideo motor responses, sensory ideo, and ideo-emotional** *amplifying the response levels and deepening the evocative experiences and sensory, physical and mental extra.*

✓ Ability to develop Phenomenon Hypnotic Analgesia and Anesthesia moderate, overall pain control, ability to walk on burning coals, traversed with pins and tolerance have contact with fire and ice.

✓ Amnesia develop the ability to forget situations, memories, events, phobias, fears and traumas.

✓ Hypnotic phenomenon Lethargy, Catalepsy and Catatonic moderate and high cataleptic limbs or entire body.

✓ Ability to maintain Hypnotic Trance with eyes open or closed and develop the ability to maintain hypnotic phenomena.

✓ **State of hyper - suggestibility** "It is a superior amplification response or downrigger the suggestive experiences or state of hyper concentration and total relaxation that is metaphorically associated with deep slumber, the latter called hypnotic trance state.

✓ Hallucinations multisensory medium, high and you moderate - visual, auditory and kinesthetic, olfactory and gustatory. (See things that really do not see, hear things that actually feel sensations, feelings and physical contacts that are not really real, smell and taste smells or tastes that do not actually exist in the real physical world do not listen)

✓ Ability to consciously control heart rhythm, deep breathing or lethargic and voluntarily control body levels body to withstand high or low temperatures.

✓ higher level of control extended trance and hypnotic phenomena and the state of somnambulism.

✓ superior ability to accept and receive direct suggestions, commands, patterns and hypnotic inductions high intensity of a circle power level Force or Authority Level "FP7" and "FP8".

✓ *Development capacity **xenoglossia** which it is the ability or paranormal phenomenon hypnotic speaking unknown languages and languages.*

✓ *Capacity **NOESIOLOGY** which it is the ability of healing with thought. Greek noesis: action of thinking, and healing therapy.*

✔ *psychographics psychic ability of a person who writes letters without being aware. The person says the words were written by the subconscious, by a spirit or supernatural forces related to hypnosis.*

✔ *Ability to develop hypnotic phenomena as regressions, distortion or disassociation of time and space, body, visual or auditory illusions, deep meditation, and for alleged mystical experiences, such as clairvoyance, psychographics, xenoglossia, the **Noesiology** and even lucid dreams, astral travel and extrasensory experiences.*

OTHER THEORIES ON HYPNOSIS

As we have been studying so far apprentice, we can deduce that hypnosis like all hypnotic phenomena that relate to it; is a state of mind, an altered state or a state of natural behavior that has existed since the origins of humanity, with different names and applications over time, but always remain in all ages the same psiconeurofisiológico phenomenon.

Today is understood HYPNOSIS different approaches as a model, a communicational style, a specific state of receptivity, a cognitive experience and a hyper-suggestible predisposition uses and optimizes own potential and internal resources possessed by each person. Currently apprentice; there is no predominant, or exclusive single theory, but rather there are a number of theories and concepts, each with its own view.

In another apprentice ideas, although hypnosis is real and absolutely practical, therapeutic and functional. Theories and postulates are not yet defined in a single particular idea is more like a set of different ideas, that complement holistic and synergistically together, from different points of views, which provide lighter and information, while new concepts through constant studies and research on this wonderful discipline are discovered. For this reason, many HYPNOSES is and remains an enigma, or one of the seven wonders of the ancient and modern psychology.

Let us study SOME OF THE MOST IMPORTANT THEORIES

1. The theory of hypnosis as Effective Communication. All hypnosis is effective communication, "feedback, feedback / stimulus response" verbal and nonverbal communication. For this theory hypnosis and all its possible applications are derived from good communication. In other words, an apprentice; for this theory, hypnosis is the ability to stimulate multi-sensory perceptions through figurative language created by the spoken word, which is ultimately that can produce alterations in our consciousness; bringing the BioRetroacción result, which is the process by which stimulate a response through a specific action, created and designed to cause a particular purpose. In other words;

2. Theory Hypnotic relaxation and concentration as. For this theory, deep relaxation and mental concentration are considered as the primary and fundamental source producing hypnosis. And why supposedly derive all other hypnotic phenomena, such as: The regressions, distortion or disassociation of time and space, body, visual or auditory illusions, deep meditation, and for alleged mystical experiences, such as clairvoyance, psychographics, xenoglossia, Noesiology and even lucid dreams, astral travel and extrasensory experiences.

3. Theory Dissociative. Dissociative theory states that there are multiple cognitive systems normally work synergistically under primary control. During hypnosis, the normally integrated with each other subsystems dissociate (separate) from each other at different scales or levels, and are capable of simultaneous and independent multiple degrees of consciousness to the suggestions and inductions declared by the hypnotist answers.

4. Psychological Regression Theory. This theory states that hypnosis is a special form of psychological regression that is characterized by a change of more primitive primary thought, and an altered increased state of consciousness through data transfer (suggestions and inductions) declared by the hypnotist or hypnotizer, which, for this theory, represents a figure of almost archetypal authority.

5. Theory socio-cognitive This theory states that hypnosis is not a unique or particular experience of a psychic phenomenon but rather is defined by the psychosocial and psicocognitivo context in which the hypnotic phenomenon occurs through fashion, belief or mental map which each participant perceives and understand the processes hypnotics, and why, consider the hypnotic responses as part of the result of induction.

6. Theory of hypnosis as a permissive state. The authoritarian approach with clinical hypnotherapists with a more traditional orientation to hypnosis CLASSIC, is the basis for the description that this theory of passive and permissive behavior that develops the subject. This theory states that the permissive individual is one that is characterized by allowing the hypnotist or grant or clinical hypnotist direct your subjective experience, expressing little or no desire to resist the orders given during the hypnosis session. This theory expects the subject (patient or participant) responds much as you can to the guidance, instruction, tips, and suggestions (inductions) direct the hypnotist, and thus, the person involved in a receptive passive and secondary role in the relationship "patient - doctor "" participant - hypnotist ". In other words, this theory,

7. hypnosis as Feedback. For this theory, or get feedback (feedback) of the senses regarding our relationship with the outside world around us, it is a process called "contrasting with reality". This process is usually so unconscious and involuntary, that we take for granted in the hypnotic sessions. This theory states that when we first enter into a state of hypnotic trance, the ongoing process of contrasting reality is markedly reduced or almost nil. When you stop the process of getting feedback or (feedback) with the outside world around him, focusing solely on their own internal processes, giving as results hypnotic phenomena, which allows the person to deflect any guidance that is out of their inner subjective experience, and this process is what characterizes most hypnotic experiences "{(but of course, hypnosis can also focus on external aspects, as applicable)}" On another idea to suspend the objective contrasting with reality the person through hypnosis, the subject is free to accept any subjective reality that suggests. The suggested reality, whether it is true or false, will determine the quality and quantity of responses ideo motor, sensory ideo, and ideo-emotional and behavioral of the person. the subject is free to accept any subjective reality that suggests. The suggested reality, whether it is true or false, will determine the quality and quantity of responses ideo motor, sensory ideo, and ideo-emotional and behavioral of the person. the subject is free to accept any subjective reality that suggests. The suggested reality, whether it is true or false, will determine the quality and quantity of responses ideo motor, sensory ideo, and ideo-emotional and behavioral of the person.

8. hypnosis as Theory of Role Playing. Socio-cognitive especially for this perspective, hypnosis as an entity separate and unique consciousness does not really exist as such. For this theory, only the HYPNOSIS occurs when someone (the patient or participant) wishes to represent it voluntarily. For this theory, (the patient or participant) does not really enter into a dimension of consciousness that differs appreciably from any other. Rather, the person or subject in question, plays an active role in what is supposed to be, or should be, and acts according to those previously established parameters. On another idea (the patient or participant) meets and follow the suggestions, and suggestions (inductions) declared by the hypnotist for a given purpose in advance to fulfill a particular purpose.

9. Hypnosis as an altered state of consciousness. This theory believes and states that the hypnotic state is a real, unique, separate and distinct from the normal state of monitors state. For this reason, this hypnotic state can be created and artificially produced by the correct process of hypnotic induction, which alters subjective and phenomenological experience of the person concerned. Thus, limiting the critical factor of the mind and mindfulness of the individual through the suggestions and inductions that are offered by the specialist hypnotist, hypnotherapist or hypnotist.

10. Biological Theories. For this theory, the strong relationship between mind and body (psyche and Somas) is clearly evident in the hypnotic interactions. And this has led to theoretical formulations that defend the existence of a biological and physiological basis in the predisposition of the person in front of hypnosis. This results in "{(the quality of existing holistic and integral relationship between the two brain hemispheres and the ultradian rhythm and hemispheric asymmetry)}" consequently resulting in the occurrence of different hypnotic phenomena in hypnosis sessions.

11 State Theory Vs. Not State the Perez-Garrido, González-Ordi and Miguel-Tobal authors argue that basic research on hypnosis have focused, among other issues, to find out what the underlying characteristics of hypnotic's processes. Most researchers are assigned to two conceptions or different paradigms about the nature of hypnosis: 1) The traditional paradigm, which assumes that hypnosis involves an altered state of consciousness, and 2) The paradigm, cognitive-behavioral or socio-cognitive, which argues that it is not necessary to resort to the concept of altered state to explain the hypnotic behavior. Let us give some examples to understand these ideas:

12.- Theory of Clinical Hypnosis. Theory CLINICAL HYPNOSIS, is based on the belief that there is a link mode of bipersonal or multipersonal relationship between patient and Hypnotherapist. HYPNOSIS CLINIC is considered a functional communication where the therapist communicates effectively with the inner world of the patient, through subjective experiences that hypnotherapist causes it through inductions and verbal suggestions, through power of the spoken word. Taking as a starting point, hypnosis clinic is the ability to communicate feelings of safety, protection, consideration, care and mutual respect. Thus, through the interpersonal relationship of effective communication, it allows the patient attenuates its defense mechanisms of the waking state and let down your guard CRITICAL FACTOR OF MIND, which finally passed these two obstacles allow the patient to achieve a state of intense physical and mental serenity. thus, achieving a deep hypnotic trance state desired by focusing on itself and the inner experiences caused by the specialist. From this perspective, hypnosis clinic will be seen as a PHENOMENON OF EFFICIENT which shows the relationship between a protected being (patient) and a protective character (hypnotherapist). a deep hypnotic trance state desired by focusing on itself and the inner experiences caused by the specialist. From this perspective, hypnosis clinic will be seen as a PHENOMENON OF EFFICIENT which shows the relationship between a protected being (patient) and a protective character (hypnotherapist). a deep hypnotic trance state desired by focusing on itself and the inner experiences caused by the specialist. From this perspective, hypnosis clinic will be seen as a PHENOMENON OF EFFICIENT which shows the relationship between a protected being (patient) and a protective character (hypnotherapist).

13.- Theory Hiper-Suggestibility. Currently this is one of the most popular theories and widespread in recent years. This theory is based on the conscious attention subject is hypnotics processes, which are closely related to certain techniques inductions and verbal suggestions strategically used by clinical hypnologist or hypnotist of theatrical show, to cause certain hypnotics phenomena the individual. As the attention of the subject (patient or participant) focuses on the power of the spoken word of the hypnotist; this eventually through verbal suggestions and hypnotic inductions is superimposed to the inner voice of the subject involved, helping to develop ideo motor responses, sensory ideo, and ideo-emotional.

14.- Theory of Social Construction Theory Role. This theory suggests that individuals (patients or participants) assume a previously preset participatory role, and thus allow the hypnotist to create in them an alternate reality SUBJECTIVE. This relationship depends on how much information has been preliminarily established between the hypnotist and the subject. This theory suggests that generally under the influence of hypnosis people become more receptive to suggestion, allowing you to create positive changes in the way they think, feel and behave the individual. Much experimental work in the field of hypnosis has shown that the subjective experiences of the hypnotized subjects can be dramatically shaped by expectations and social nuances. "{(This view can usually be misunderstood. The theory of social construction and role theory does not discredit the claim that hypnotized individuals are really experiencing real effects of suggestion. Only it states that the mechanisms which carry out these actions, are partly built psycho-social and are not necessarily informed only in a state of altered consciousness)} ".

15.- Scientific Theory and Physiological Aspects. Thanks to the research that has been done through the years about hypnosis have been discovered neurophysiological processes and brain areas that are actively involved in all known hypnotic phenomena. Among the most striking brain areas that are activated in the hypnotic processes we can mention the following: The dorsolateral prefrontal cortex and cingulate cortex. Areas related to the processes of attention and awareness. 1 The prefrontal cortex that is an integrative area that relates to the planning, selective attention, and modulation of other brain functions (usually via inhibition). 2nd The other major area involved is the cingulate cortex which is formed as part of the limbic system involved in different functions such as reward, error detection, attention, motivation and especially emotions. In fact, these brain areas are actively involved in many other aspects related to human experience and behavior. Other scientific studies have shown that hypnosis has also been linked to hemispheric asymmetry; related to the cerebral hemispheres. These findings are argued in some research suggesting that responses hypnotic processes are associated more to the right hemisphere of the brain. Since these responses are more related to cognitive processes, creative, intuitive and non-verbal thoughts produced in this hemisphere. They are actively involved in many other aspects related to human experience and behavior. Other scientific studies have shown that hypnosis has also been linked to hemispheric asymmetry; related to the cerebral hemispheres. These findings are argued in some research suggesting that responses hypnotic processes are associated more to the right hemisphere of the brain. Since these responses are more related to cognitive processes, creative, intuitive and non-verbal thoughts produced in this hemisphere. They are actively involved in many other aspects related to human experience and behavior. Other scientific studies have shown that hypnosis has also been linked to hemispheric asymmetry; related to the cerebral hemispheres. These findings are argued in some research suggesting that responses hypnotic processes are associated more to the right hemisphere of the brain. Since these responses are more related to cognitive processes, creative, intuitive and non-verbal thoughts produced in this hemisphere. related to the cerebral hemispheres. These findings are argued in some research suggesting that responses hypnotic processes are associated more to the right hemisphere of the brain. Since these responses are more related to cognitive processes, creative, intuitive and non-verbal thoughts produced in this hemisphere. related to the cerebral hemispheres. These findings are argued in some research suggesting that responses hypnotic processes are associated more to the right hemisphere of the brain. Since these responses are more related to cognitive processes, creative, intuitive and non-verbal thoughts produced in this hemisphere.

IN CONCLUSION: Our comprehensive review of the various existing theories of hypnosis; We have shown that, even today there are many unknowns and important questions unresolved. But the most important thing to consider is; which has been shown again and again, with every theory that hypnosis is real. And there are broad areas of common agreement among all researchers and theorists on the subject. In conclusion: We can affirm then that the field of hypnosis continue to progress through scientific studies and coupling between rival theories. During this research process, the study of hypnosis will continue to enrich the broad field of psychology, providing new insights into cognitive, behavioral and relational dimensions of human experience.

CHAPTER III: MYTHS, LEGENDS AND SPECULATION ABOUT MODERN HYPNOSIS

Well champions, we have reached one of the most important sections of the theoretical framework. Once we have understood the development of the historical and evolutionary context of hypnosis through the centuries, we have understood the multiple definitions and theories of hypnosis, NOW is of vital apprentice importance, understand the reality and the perjuries behind the MYTHS, LEGENDS and SPECULATIONS AROUND HYPNOSIS. Since knowing and understanding what are the most frequent misrepresentations around hypnosis, will help us to be able to eliminate the falsely infused fears and insecurities or mistrust that exists in the minds of people. Since, if fear is present to some degree, whether the person is aware of it or not, it can negatively affect the process of hypnosis, since people could unconsciously put up resistance, and this is something we should avoid.

Before continuing apprentice, I will clarify a little more the term hypnosis. Because as is well known, the practice of hypnosis MODERN is a masterful art of personal excellence and discipline extraordinarily effective therapies and hypnotic sessions; but nevertheless, it has been misinterpreted and questioned by many people over the years, mainly due to bad ideas and misconceptions created by the ritualistic use and theatrics of ancient HYPNOSIS, as well as the negative influence of certain films Hollywood, celebrity magazines, newspapers critics exaggerated articles of people with ignorance on the subject, certain religious beliefs, and even the practice of unscrupulous people who use hypnosis or used inappropriately, anti-ethical and anti-professional.

The general idea and the most common perception people have of HYPNOSIS CLINIC and especially the show is the complete domination of the mind, and absolute control of the hypnotist or hypnotherapist to another human being; these ideas are wrong and completely false. That to have nothing to do with real hypnosis.

As I explained earlier in the first chapter, the word "trance", "hypnosis" or "hypnotic patterns" can be misinterpreted, and even certain associations or even arouse negative feelings in some people who know the subject. When in fact the "Trance", the "HYPNOSIS" and "Hypnotic Patterns" is a discipline and a psychotherapeutic science proven through the years, and applied scientific and professionally over time by some of the leading hypnotherapists specialists, influential and renowned history.

Including the renowned Dr. Milton H. Erickson pioneer of modern clinical hypnosis, creator of the call or Milton Ericksonian Hypnosis Method *(Principles of which we have already discussed earlier in this later chapters).*

So; clarified this point, we can remember how we have been taught during all the preceding paragraphs, the real HYPNOSIS THERAPEUTICS, is the science that allows us to go directly to the subconscious mind of people and to pass the critical factor of the mind through the hypnotic process "{(guidance, instruction, tips, and suggestions (inductions) direct declared by the hypnotist as well as metaphors, parables, allegories, stories, tales, narratives and figurative language"}), allowing participants potentially stimulate AC subjective reality helping develop responses ideo motor, sensory ideo,

Making all these elements in a holistic, comprehensive and synergistic manner in a completely effective and very effective to achieve the trance state HYPNOTIC DESIRED tool in which the individual enters an altered state of intense physical and mental serenity. Amplified the Psycho-answers and deepening the evocative experiences a state of "hyper-suggestibility", "hyper-creativity", "hyper-imagination", "hyper concentration" and "hyper-relaxation" that allows them to experience individual's personal transformations a more efficient, effective and simpler way so that if performing the same hypnotic procedure in alertness or wakefulness (BETA WAVES between 14 to 28 Hz or cycles per second).

Recall apprentice; the unconscious mind that we possess all people, is where neural programming and mental maps of individuals are stored. And with them, they are also codes of ethics, as well as the strictest moral values of people, allowing them to live according to the highest standards focused on their moral principles. It is for this reason that even if a person is in a complete state of hypnotic trance, if you give an order that is contrary to its ethical principles and moral values, this is not going to accept, because your subconscious mind knows what it's good or not.

Since your unconscious mind, is alert and knows what is good, and recognizes what is bad. And the subconscious mind fence would never do something against their code of ethics and moral principles! It also happens when the hypnotic command goes against either of their ingrained beliefs or any other idea fence against an act that threatens the survival of the individual.

> **_NOTE_**: _It is clear, that like any other discipline; there are people who, through practice, experience and continuous preparation develop certain skills that go beyond what is experienced by people You average, allowing them to take their skills to a level higher than normal._ **_Let me give AN EXAMPLE_**_: Perhaps many people practice meditation or disciplines, right? But the preparation and delivery of a Tibetan Buddhist monk or allows you to reach a much higher level, what would people come or You average. And this skill acquired with practice, experience and continuous preparation allows them to Buddhist monks and Tibetan monks reach what they call the state of enlightenment._
>
> _In hypnosis it is the same. Practice, experience and continuous preparation allows certain Hypnotists, Hypnotists, hypnotists and hypnotherapists Clinical, increase your circle of power and force level or level of authority to a higher level (FP's) enabling them to develop their hypnotic skills to the next level, (my friend to another level) understand?_
>
> _This allows them to create direct and indirect orders, inductions and suggestions for optimal and effective way, gradually rising in grades HYPNOSIS. That is, they manage to ascend from the circle of power and force level or level of authority to a higher level FP0 and FP1, until FP5 and higher, which enables them to produce certain hypnotic phenomena that would otherwise be impossible._

Clarified this point, I now want to share with you another definition of hypnosis to reinforce what has been learned up to this point, and allow the we move ahead subject matter of the book especially this chapter.

Hypnosis as an apprentice we learned so far, is a state of mind, state of trance known as **state** "Hyper - suggestibility", ie, amplifier or downrigger response suggestive of experiences that activates a group of attitudes generated through a discipline called hypnotism. Hypnosis is a state of hyper then concentration and relaxation akin to sleep metaphorically speaking that is achieved through SUGGESTION and commands or PATTERNS OF PERSUASION used by the therapist or hypnotist. these commands and persuasive patterns of a series of verbal instructions and oral suggestions along with other techniques verbal induction or conduction produces the hypnotic phenomenon is usually composed.

The use of hypnosis for therapeutic purposes, as applies NLP, and particularly in this book is known as metamodel, hypnosis, hypnotics ericksoniana patterns or hypnosis.

As I discussed earlier, the ignorance of the art of hypnosis and persuasion as proven science, sometimes tends to confuse people who know little of the applicability of this methodology in the various branches of psychotherapy. Consequently, resulting in many people think that the hypnotist has amazing supernatural or magical powers up, which can cause fear when being hypnotized by a professional. The biggest culprit of these myths, as I referred to earlier, is the popular culture where Mesmer is often seen as a magician who has supreme powers, able to take over weak minds of people, and all this is very from the truth. That is a myth, an unfounded belief and an opposing view to the truth.

For this reason, know the myths surrounding hypnosis is important because it will help us time to break those mental barriers limiting and self-saboteur's thoughts that people have when it comes to hypnosis, hypnotism or hypnotic trance.

Good champions and champions to learn more about this wonderful art, we will know the most popular myths surrounding hypnosis in its many variations, so without further ado let's begin.

MYTH 1. Hypnotists have magical, mystical and special powers. This first statement is completely false. Since the practice of hypnosis once you know its principles it is "very simple and learning" so simple that anyone who provides, study it carefully and practice may develop. This is something that knows everything Mesmer expert; and it is for this reason that there are some Mesmer (hypnotists shows or hypnotists Clinical) to give the HYPNOSIS an air of "mystery" or "professionalism" and try to convince people (participants or patients) that hypnosis is something very "difficult" that only a few who have the "Don Magic or Special Power" or "studies or university degree" are the only ones empowered to achieve these phenomena HYPNOTICS on individuals (participants or patients) involved in their sessions. I Reaffirmed "This myth is false." Since it's not really DON nor Titration what makes you an excellent hypnotist, but the preparation, discipline, constant practice and knowledge of different techniques and methodologies, which, together with the conscious, pro-active, voluntary and participative people, are ultimately the key pillars that allow you to professionally develop this discipline in any of the two fields mentioned.

So why all this confusion? Let me share with you some examples in both cases, to understand the root cause has been the emergence and popularization of this myth: To begin, I confess that I have personally met many Mesmer (hypnotists Shows) my colleagues, surrounding the art of hypnosis an air of "occult", "secrecy" and "mystery" for people "normal" on stage do not see that really is the hypnotic procedure. "Because if you see, many of these (hypnotist's theater or hypnotists Shows)" lose their supernatural power ". So, the professional hypnotist says wise and categorically that it is the "power of your mind" that allows hypnotize the other person, and that only a privileged few, those who are born with this supposed "DON" are the only ones capable hypnotize ... (Les reveal something, I understand why they do it. it's part of the show, creating the scenario that uncertainty in people and generate those expectations increases levels of hyper-suggestibility because these beliefs psychologically help participants to be more receptive to the inductions and suggestions of the hypnotist. what creates these dramatic hypnotic phenomena that both surprise people ... and because I know? ... for myself, my dear readers, in my beginnings in this hypnotic ART also he performed exhibitions of street hypnosis and hypnosis show in theaters and shows, which allowed me to see and understand for myself how these myths, together with certain advertising strategies, I gave such an excellent result in the viewer's mind.

The first example, on the one hand; On the other hand, I have also had the opportunity to meet and share with other colleagues of mine (hypnotists Clinical), those who work as professionals Doctors or Hypnotherapists, that even today, still surround their work physician-scientist of certain "psychological barriers" to that normal patients or ordinary people not "acquire these therapeutic techniques" irresponsibly. This time, these "psychological barriers" created were the need to supposedly study these "very fat books and encyclopedias" full of theory of the "most complex concepts of hypnosis" that, instead of encouraging new entrants, they create more uncertainties than answers. Another of the "psychological barriers" are "

Now let's move to this second place and understand why these "psychological barriers". This principle is logical to understand, that is, it's easy to understand why doctors and specialists feed this myth. Since this "professional jealousy" is what keeps the THERAPEUTIC HYPNOSIS away from the unscrupulous, unethical people and anti-professionals who could exercise this art or discipline without prior adequate preparation or without college or qualifications required for this purpose. Recall that hypnosis clinic should be studied professionally, ie it must receive a tuition university certificate or diploma to exercise therapy, professionally and ethically.

<u>**NOTE**</u>: *It should be noted that although each of the points or above examples are essential and vital to understand when making a hypnotic show or practice clinical hypnosis therapeutically. Actually, there is no special or magical about either specialty power.* Moreover, if we talk about something special or magical about hypnosis show or clinical hypnosis, it is the gift of self to be hypnotizable person. Which is, I repeat and repeat again, it is this gift, the ability to be hypnotized, and this wonderful quality the people themselves have received verbal suggestions or hypnotic inductions by the hypnotist or hypnotherapist. Since we are professional hypnotists simply a guide who directs the hypnotic experience of people through the tools and appropriate to generate the desired state of hypnotic trance methodologies.

MYTH 2. <u>Only a select few are hypnotizable</u>. This second myth is also totally false! Why? Because everyone is hypnotizable to a lesser or greater degree, depending on the predisposition, the will and exerted influence that has on the subject in question (I'll share some ideas, the first of it is that we have more inclination to let us persuade by people we trust authority. for example, a child is more influenced by his mother, as well as the patient is from your doctor). Just what happens is that it is easier or faster or more suggestible for some people be hypnotized (programmed) than for others. YOU EXPLAIN WHY ...Hypnotic Trance is a natural state of the body, which actually happens every day, every moment and in various ways or forms in our daily lives, only we do not realize it consciously.

*(**P**or example by following the example above, the child is mesmerized by his mother when orients, guides and directs its development "If the mother program principles and values from childhood to his son when he says he is a good boy, what you are doing is setting them {hypnotizing} for the young believe and half that fence grow has these deeply rooted teaching your subconscious mind, in your thinking, feeling and acting "the same is true in the opposite case; Imagine what would happen if instead of teaching principles and values to children, parents, as unfortunately in some homes decreed about their children who are losers, failures and useless,*

HYPNOSIS IS THAT? Of course, it is) ...

Keep in mind that Hypnosis is such a natural psychological process of every human being, maybe you already have entered HYPNOTIC TRANCE OFTEN again and again; in your childhood or youth, without even have noticed it. Or maybe, even now, you might've hypnotized (positively programming you these teachings) As you read this chapter carefully. *(Para continue and get back to the topic, let me share you another idea; continuing the above example the doctor and patient. "Every time the doctor prescribes a drug (treatment) to the patient and tells him, with him, this will improve your health; predisposes (program or hypnotizes) to make it so. But there is also the opposite case, imagine what would happen if the doctor made a mistake prescription and carelessness or negligence as also happened, tells the patient that his illness is recorded and will not improve, this doctor inadvertently is programming it {hypnotizing} for the patient to believe and respond to this situation, even if it was only a diagnostic error "... THIS IS HYPNOSIS? Sure, it is and certainly very common.*

Remember that hypnosis is a skill or natural ability that have developed in the course of our lives, making us more suggestible} *{Hypnotizable at all times and on many occasions, we are aware of them or not ...* Let me give you some other examples: The same situation hypnosis or "altered state of consciousness" or hypnotic state and repeated INVOLUNTARY happens very regularly in our daily lives ***FOR EXAMPLE*** *When we see a good movie, and we go into the history and the argument it so much that without realizing it ends the film by immersing both the plot; so, they were literally mesmerized by the film, we begin to recreate in our minds the same feelings, experiences, situations, events, thoughts, feelings, ideals and even the emotional states of the protagonists; to such an extent that we experience at that time their same emotions, whether those of fear, horror, suspense, drama, pain, sadness, joy, happiness, love, passion, excitement, sensuality and even desire. With such intensity, as if we were we the protagonists of the film HYPNOSIS IS THAT? Of course).*

<u>Another good example would be</u> When someone tells a fascinating story, or tells us about an event or situation that has lived a person, and describes it with such intensity, passion and emotion, we hear we begin to be able to vividly imagine those same emotions or circumstances narrated in the situation, and recreate in our powerful subconscious mind every event of the story as if we were living and experiencing ourselves personally at that precise moment. That is, [At that moment, the person who listens attentively to the story, is so absorbed in the story, which goes into a state of trance ALFA or "altered states of consciousness" without even realizing it or notice]. Now I ask *THIS IS HYPNOSIS? Of course, it is itself too. True?*

Anyway, my dear readers, as we saw in the previous examples, check and at every moment, at all times and in every place or circumstance which we live, we generate a lot of multisensory situations that we produce or generate a response UNCONSCIOUS in our bodies and that we call HYPNOSIS STATE OF CONSCIOUSNESS ALTERED STATE OF TRANCE HYPNOTIC or involuntary. And all these multisensory stimuli happen within us internally, without even noticing them. All that happens is that you do not even realize you were this reality; that is, you never knew you possessed those skills and hypnotic qualities always; and for that reason, until now you had not realized this innate power of the mind consciously you have in your favor.

> In short, the MYTH 2. Only a select few are hypnotizable is totally and completely false. Because as we show all the people are and can be hypnotizable in one way or another; and all persons have entered a sort of altered state of consciousness or HYPNOTIC STATE OF TRANCE INVOLUNTARY to a lesser or greater degree; consciously and unconsciously we have been aware of it or not.
>
> **YOU HAVE ALWAYS PRESENT**: *YES, you can learn to hypnotize, anyone, anytime and anywhere. The issue is not, if you go into hypnosis, the question is, when you enter. Since everyone is hypnotizable if you know the "how" and "what" answers.*

MYTH 3. Only people with little will can be hypnotizable or just Hypnotize the Weak-Minded People Can Be.

We question this false myth ... Until the next question Have you ever thought about the number of people using self-hypnosis, positive suggestions or power of your mind as a means to improve or outdo themselves? In fact, it has been shown scientifically proven time and again that the most creative, intuitive, full of imagination and self-reliant people enter into trances HYPNOTIC much faster, more effectively and in a way more powerful than those individuals who have doubts or lack of creativity and imagination. Since I repeat, it has been shown scientifically proven that an open mind and a positive attitude is much more powerful, intuitive and resourceful, that endless chances limitless much greater and extraordinary than the average person opens.

le champions and champions, that people who go into a hypnotic trance state are not weak-minded in any way; On the contrary, one can say that people who enter hypnosis are more open minded, receptive, willing and ingenious. In other words, they are more susceptible (capable, able, willing, skillful) and responsive to hypnotic trance state. That is, they are more sensitive and lend to the suggestions of the hypnotist and inductions people. And this quality so extraordinarily wonderful my dear readers is a skill, natural talent or innate talent. More than a defect, is an attention span that we should all want to develop.

> *In short,* <u>**3. MYTH PEOPLE WITH ONLY WILL BE hypnotizable LITTLE OR You can only hypnotize WEAK MINDED PEOPLE**</u>**.** It is completely and totally false ...

MITO No. 4. Under Hypnosis are totally vulnerable. give the lie to this

another false myth ... Hypnosis has never been, nor ever will be a vulnerable situation where you lose the absolute control under the influence of the hypnotist, as many people mistakenly believe. Since we have to remember what I have emphasized in previous sections that even while under a state of deep hypnotic trance, our consciousness is always active and latent retain our values and our MORALES highest ethical standards. So, no one, nothing can induce us to take action, say anything or do anything for what we have not given our approval and prior authorization; because everything can be done through hypnosis or HYPNOSIS CLINIC SPECTACLE is only and only with the voluntary and participatory consent of the person concerned. All that can be achieved through hypnosis, it is that we do IF THEY WANT and if we chose; It is to do, feel, think or act in the way that the theater hypnotist, the hypnotist shows, clinical hypnotist or hypnotherapist what specialist suggests. As long as we agree to it voluntarily, especially if we know that is good and useful for us.

Recall that the subconscious mind that we possess all people, is where our neural settings are stored and with them, are also codes of ethics, as well as the strictest moral values of people; allowing them to live according to the highest standards focused on their moral principles. It is for this reason, my dear readers that even when a person is in a complete state of hypnotic trance, if given an order that is contrary to its ethical principles and moral values, this would never agree to it and could never accept it, because your subconscious mind knows what is good for us or not.

We must always remember that our unconscious mind is alert at every moment of our life, and she knows what is good for us, and immediately recognize what is bad. And the subconscious mind fence would never do something against their code of ethics and moral principles! ... It also happens when a hypnotic order goes against either of our deeply held beliefs or any other ideal we have, if order is contrary to these high standards we have registered the subconscious mind is activated in alert mode, rejecting the order automatically, as this will never allow to do or perform an act that threatens the survival of the individual.

> *In short,* <u>**MITO No. 4. ARE TOTALLY under hypnosis VULNERABLE**</u> It is completely and totally false. Because as we have already clarified on several occasions, under any hypnotic trance are not going to do anything you do not want to do, why do you ask? Well the reason is because even in a state of deep hypnosis, which as you know are going to always be aware at all times of induction, allowing you to listen and follow directions, suggestions and direct suggestions declared by the hypnotist, hypnotist, hypnotist or clinical hypnotherapist Since we are simply a guide who directs the hypnotic experience of people through the tools and appropriate to generate the desired state of hypnotic trance methodologies.

MYTH 5. I can stay asleep forever. give the lie to this myth once and for all. Keep in mind that although the term hypnosis comes from the Greek term (Hypnos) which means dream, the real state experienced in a hypnotic trance, it is more akin to a state of relaxation or meditation in which we are always aware at all times what happens around us. THEN THERE BECAUSE THIS FEAR falling asleep? Let me explain briefly ...

Hypno-SIS to come from the Greek word (Hypnos) which means sleep is associated symbolically and metaphorically to numbness, sleep or lethargy but remember that the term hypnosis is only an allegorical reference GREEK MYTHOLOGY (Hypnos) and EGYPTIAN ANCIENT PRACTICES that are associated with (Sleep Temples Egyptians) practiced in ancient times. That means that, in actual practice, modern hypnosis has nothing to do with the act of "falling asleep or doze SOUND" literally.

As has been scientifically proven hypnosis is "A normal physiological state of man where certain similar physiological phenomena REM sleep occur, which, when activated by the suggestions and hypnotic inductions declared by (hypnotist, hypnotizer, clinical hypnologist or hypnotherapist), allows the appearance of answers ideo motor, ideo sensory, and ideo-emotional, but the subject in question always remains awake and alert at all times, only in a much higher state of relaxation, meditation and concentration the waking state.

While it is true that certain features of REM sleep state come into play in the hypnotic process, it is important to note as we have already clarified earlier that the state of hypnotic trance is very different to normal physiological sleep we know as the act of (SLEEP) ". Since I repeat, at any time during the procedure, people in the state of hypnotic trance fall into something like a deep sleep, much less literally sleep.

MYTH No. 6 Can Hypnosis Mentally Impair a negative way or Hypnosis Can be dangerous in occasions? This myth is one of the most interesting; For this reason, leave it in last place to explain and understand clearly favorable and unfavorable balanced, negative or positive and reality or fiction of this myth. To begin we can state categorically that the hypnotic act is not dangerous in itself. Experience through the years, and hundreds of scientific medical studies show us decisively that you cannot make an individual (patient or participant) under hypnosis adopt conduct contrary to your moral ethics, principles and values, religious beliefs, morals, ideals or any other thoughts, feelings or actions that violates dignity or put your life at risk or endangered. Consider that the (street hypnotist, the hypnotist show,

If for example a street hypnotist in one of his presentations street manages to make one of its participants fingers, hands or feet sticking, it is because the same participant agreed to the suggestions freely, realizing that these very popular

hypnotic phenomena in this types of presentations are conducted through the voluntary participation of the person itself, who know that is only part of a mental game can be swayed by bringing experience as a result favorably achieve the desired hypnotic phenomenon. Similarly, if a hypnotist show gets a subject the public to behave like a dog, cat or any other animal, it is because the person in question knows intuitively and unconsciously that it is a game in which he is the protagonist;

So, if you have to take into account, and I emphasize so important it is. It is that no street hypnotist or hypnotist show should for any reason, reason or circumstance diagnostics or treat diseases without prior knowledge and be authorized for this purpose, as this is solely and exclusively for clinical and hypnotherapists hypnotist's specialist who are empowered and qualified for such therapies and procedures. It is important to note at this point that any diagnosis or treatment should only be carried out by specialists in the subject such as they are, psychiatrists, doctors, psychologists and hypnotherapists. Neither the coach nor the trainer in NLP are empowered to diagnose or treat diseases unless they are properly qualified and authorized to do so,

<u>MYTH No. 7 can always remember our experiences and make REGRESSIONS the past when we are hypnotized</u>. Before explaining this myth, it is important to clarify that certain disciplines and specialists to perform these hypnotic phenomena called REGRESSIONS (which are able to produce on the subject (patient or participant) the opportunity to "experiences of the field of hypnosis past "and stimulate memory with his memories stored in your subconscious mind, to bring the present with a specific purpose and a specific objective previously established between the person and the hypnotist).

Keeping this idea in mind; it is vital to be clear, that sometimes the hypnotist or hypnotherapist SPECIALIST REGRESSIONS if you can take us through a hypnosis session; back in time, in order to find some detail of interest in our past and bring it into the present. That is to say; the here and now. And this happens mostly because the hypnotherapist has been able to reach the fragments sheltered or deeper layers of our subconscious mind where memory resides. Which it is the bank where it is stored thoughts and memories we have forgotten. And what specifically does the hypnotist, is back those memories, thoughts or memories from past to present; allowing revive them, remember them, access them and experience them again as memories, more present thoughts or memories. And so, work towards it to achieve a purpose or goal previously established between the parties.

In this sense, hypnosis if you can help us remember certain experiences of the past when we are hypnotized and bringing them to the present with a specific purpose. BUT WHAT YOU CAN DO HYPNOSIS is lead us to relive a past life or remember events, facts and situations that have actually occurred.

To recapitulate: Apprentices; the hypnotic state is no risk, since hypnosis is a natural state of every human being. If there is any possibility of danger at some point; this could only be married, inadvertently, through unauthorized, negligent and incompetent practice by a hypnotist, Hypnotist, hypnotist and hypnotherapist; exercising the profession without the background needed for making or without a university degree required, if applicable.

__Psychological risks__ Apprentice; If you're not a psychiatrist, psychologist or hypnotherapist entitled, collegial and certificate and you lack information about the past of the person (you can accentuate an imbalance, but not provoke him.) (You can also provide an excuse to fall into a latent imbalance).

For this reason, it is not advisable to practice clinical hypnosis without: Have maintained a previous interview with the subject, have made the medical report, read and complete the therapeutic script with the patient, completing and reviewing the contract or posthypnotic agreement to keep in mind the goals they want to achieve with the session, deepening the reason for the consultation or session, ask questions on the subject to locate possible psychological and physiological problems, if any, detect fears, traumas, phobias, expectations, desires and interests, etc. Above all, always be sure to first have sufficient background needed and university degree required to practice ethically and professionally.

IN CONCLUSION: There is no inherent danger in hypnosis, but slight risks involved in the vast majority of the (incompetence, ineptitude, inexperience or inability) of the hypnotist, hypnotist, hypnotist or hypnotherapist clinical). For this reason, any risk can be avoided with a simple interview or therapeutic script with the subject (patient) or a brief pre-hypnotic chat with (participant) thereby treating, collect as much of facts or events in person's life, starting from the most general to the most specific. So, we would avoid these slight risks; that of course, if you can commit; as in any other specialty, career or discipline.

Do you understand what I'm saying? In doing all this my apprentice, you'll not only prevent any problems with time, but above all you can come on and cover any expectation, positioning yourself as an expert and specialist in the field; consolidate your image as Hypnotist, Hypnotist, hypnotist or hypnotherapist. It is clear that having a profile of the staff concerned who go to work, you will have more advantages, if not carry out with these initial procedures do I know you understand?

You are an apprentice agreement, which, having more information, more likely to have success in carrying out your therapeutic clinical hypnosis sessions and more likely to have success to make your shows of street hypnosis or show. Are you clear on this truth? REMEMBER: A good professional always tries to collect as many facts, information or important in the life of the person concerned events, and must do, from the general to the specific.

Good **LEARNERS**, we have **Ended with the Third Chapter**! Where we learned about the *Myths, legends and speculations around the modern HYPNOSIS*. You've come a long way, I hope you're learning a lot "And it's just the beginning of this great book about hypnosis" Remember *"If you have any questions, you can "write directly to me Email"*.

Good "apprentice dear reader" I want to thank you for purchasing this book that I wrote especially for you; I'm glad, to be your mentor and master teacher in this great art of hypnosis. The final test of the book "The power of hypnosis" will you have learned to master the essential principles to generate a state of Trance Hypnotic led by hypnosis.

(I'll share more information with you, below) I mention something very personal, you know me personally, I love teaching hypnosis is one of my greatest passions. But do and to perform all the extraordinary things that can be achieved through hypnosis, as are lucid dreams, astral travel, body experiences and hypnotic phenomena among other things. Which at first may seem like something difficult, complicated or even incredible; well yes, it is true, a little, but only at the beginning here =) "We know that home is." But I assure you, that you too can master this hypnotic art completely, because I think teach you how, and when you start to live your own experiences will be very curious and interesting for you, you'll see ^ _ ^ Well I hope soon to have your own news! ...

MásterCoach.YlichTarazona@gmail.com
http://www.reingenieriamentalconpnl.com

"Success is not a one-day event, it is a lifelong process is repeated. You can be a winner in his life if he tries. BECAUSE YOU ARE A WINNER born and from the moment of conception ... Remember: Successful people engage in activities that allow them to win from time to time; because they know that both the triumph, victory and conquest are habits that should constantly develop in their lifestyle ... Successful people; Also, they keep in mind that it is also losing wins. Because they know that every failure brings them closer to their purpose and that every defeat strengthens and teaches them what to improve. In After; both triumphs and defeats, are so important for success, that when we learn from them we become stronger and worthy of living that style and extraordinary quality of life for which we have both strive day after day. "- YLICH TARAZONA. -

CHAPTER IV: ESSENTIAL PRINCIPLES TO START USING HYPNOSIS

Congratulations champions and champions, we have come to the practical part, from now deepen what you need to learn to become an excellent hypnotist. So far, we have studied the development of historical and evolutionary context of hypnosis through the ages, we have understood the many definitions and theories that exist about hypnosis, we learned about the importance of understanding the reality and perjury behind the myths, legends and speculation about hypnosis. Now we will study the ESSENTIAL PRINCIPLES TO START USING HYPNOSIS professionally both in the field of Street Hypnosis and show as well as the clinical and therapeutic hypnosis.

To start practicing all hypnosis techniques, Suggestive PATTERNS, inductions and hypnotic commands you'll be learning then I recommend you start practicing with small groups of 3 or 6 people as fences learn each technique. At first it recommended that people who decide to start your practices are known and with whom you feel comfortable sharing these new skills that you're acquiring. Intend to practice with small groups of 3 or 6 people, it is that you can receive positive feedback; that is, effective feedback, in order to improve your techniques and methodologies hypnotic each day, while going subsequently incorporating the suggestive patterns, inductions and hypnotic commands to your repertoire,

After each practice of repeated exercises sometimes with people you've chosen to start your training period, it is important hurdles evaluating your progress through your own observations as well as effective feedback or positive feedback you receive from your collaborators.

Once you already own a domain of different hypnotic techniques, you should begin to implement and take action immediately with real people in different contexts or situations. As this will allow you to be developing the necessary experience and the hypnotic skills that will take you to become excellent hypnotist who you want and you can become. Remember to always apply in your sessions clinical or therapeutic hypnosis, or your events show of street hypnosis or show as many possible techniques to remember, since this is the only way that angers developing experiences and professionalism in the competent Domino is this wonderful supreme art of hypnosis.

Recommendations to consider each hypnosis session:

- Maintain: All the techniques and methodologies that you have done well, and continue to apply them on subsequent opportunities that will arise. Remember that practice and constant repetition is the mother of teaching. One of the ways we have to perfect our techniques and methodologies is regular evaluation of our actions in each practice session hypnosis show or event show. Because every time we evaluate us, allows us to internalize the model we used to repeat the same results more excellent the next time you perform the same technique.

- ACTIVATE: Anything you could see miss, and you did not make at the meeting or previous event. It is important that every time you make a clinical hypnosis session or a hypnotic show, then you evaluate what you did right, and what probably could have done better. As this will allow you to internalize and deepen your subconscious mind technique you used; allowing in this way, keep adding to your repertoire that you might have omitted, but if you had done or had tried, I was helped make the technique more effectively and efficiently as possible.

- OFF: Everything you did in the exercise, practice, clinical hypnosis session hypnosis show or spectacle you should not have done. As in the previous steps, this point will help you evaluate what you did in a particular therapeutic hypnosis session or event, you should not have done, or you might have missed. The purpose of this part of the exercise is that once you've assessed fairly, and have identified those points that should not have added to your sessions or show; then let you go eliminating anything that is unnecessary or surplus in actual practice in the future application of hypnosis exercises with a person.

This exercise or three-step process [HOLD - ON and OFF] will serve you to go slowly perfecting your hypnotic and persuasive skills. At the same time that will allow you to observe how they respond different people well be these (patients or participants), to the persuasive verbal suggestions or hypnotic oral inductions transmits them and communicate them to generate the hypnotic trance state desired in each context or situation which you perform hypnosis.

Principles to consider before starting a hypnosis session clinic or HYPNOSIS SHOW SPECTACLE.

Before starting to hypnotize a person, we must first begin performing a series of pre-hypnotic's protocols that allow us to significantly increase our cash success rate:

ESTABLISH HARMONY, RAPPORT AND Pacing: To achieve this, the first thing we do is clearly explain to our subject matter (patient or participant) who is and who is not hypnosis. As well as explain that you will feel or experience before, during and after the session or hypnosis show; and previously establish a close relationship between you beyond trust, so that the subject (patient or participant) allows us to access that part of your unconscious mind which is empowering them to be more relevant to the suggestions and inductions that we suggest. Thus, the subject (patient or participant) participates actively in the session or hypnosis show, without putting any psychological resistance to hypnotic commands or orders are suggesting them.

DISCONNECTION OR DISSOCIATION: The next step is to disconnect the subject (patient or participant) of the conscious part of your brain (namely, logic or rational part of your mind) of the unconscious part (ie, the suggestibility of your mind). To do this, we must begin our therapy sessions or events of street hypnosis (AS APPLICABLE) with small test exercises to prove their reaction, response, disposition and suggestibility orders before we teach them. Among the most common basic exercises that are recommended we could mention Fingers Magnetic Hands Magnetic Hands Directional Up - Down, Elevation or levitation Brazos, fall back, Catalepsy Eye, arms and legs among many others that can help us get this dissociation, and finally achieve our goal.

INTRODUCTION OF Inductions: Once done prior verification of suggestibility, we can move forward slowly in our process of hypnotic trance, beginning to use a wide variety of different verbal inductions, accompanied by hypnotic commands, suggestions and persuasive patterns that allow us to finally go running to the subject (patient or participant) to enter the desired hypnotic trance state and mental state of readiness PRE-AND POS HYPNOTIC we want to achieve with the person in question.

Induction Hypnotic is the verbal process by which the hypnotist establishes, promotes, directs and suggest the person through the power of the spoken word, to enter the subject (patient or participant) to the desired state of hypnotic trance. In other words, Hypnotic Induction is the most effective means by which the hypnotist says verbally and prepares the mental conditions required in the process of hypnosis trance medium occurs. That is, the (Hypnotic Phenomena).

In another idea, we can say that hypnotic induction can be defined as psychological processes or mental procedures HYPNOSIS necessary to bring a person to the state of hypnotic trance desired through the power of the spoken word declared by the verbal suggestions and oral inductions communicate them to the subject (patient or participant). The State of Trance Hypnotic is the state of increased suggestion or suggestibility, during which the powers of the mind criticism or critical of the mind are reduced, and subjects (patients or participants) are more likely and receptive to accept commands, patterns, suggestions, inductions, direct orders and suggestions declared by the hypnotist.

Then I will explain some of the most important to consider when starting to induce hypnotic states basic elements. There are dozens of principles in the course of this book, but I will highlight only the most essential and necessary to multiply our success rate:

most important to keep in mind when starting to induce trance states Hypnotic basic elements.

AUTHORITY: Any kind of suggestion, subliminal command, hypnotic induction, request or pray direct and indirect; It is even much better and work more effectively while awake even when performed by a person in authority. FOR EXAMPLE: If a stranger sees you sitting on a park bench, and asks you to get up to sit him or her - Would you? Undoubtedly not true ... But now imagine the same situation, and try to imagine this time, the person who asks you to get up from the bench to sit someone in authority is recognized, famous, important and relevant to you. In this new situation, you probably true Seder the bank - if true ... Why? Because it represents an authority figure or important to you. [For in the field of hypnosis it is exactly the same]. That is to say, we stand before people as an authority in the field of hypnosis; in other words, we introduce ourselves as expert hypnotists to our audience, viewers, customers or patients, for our suggestions or inductions have greater strength to the subject in question.

REPETITION: We must be repeated several times, repeatedly, in different ways and in different ways the mental states that we induce and generate the minds of people (patients or participants) who would perform the session or hypnotic show. FOR EXAMPLE: If we want the subject (patient or participant) into a state of deep relaxation trance, not enough that only we tell SLEEP, sleep or relax to produce the expected hypnotic phenomenon ... For this to really happen, we must continually repeatedly bombard your subconscious mind with verbal suggestions, subliminal commands, hypnotic inductions and direct and indirect orders that allow them to induce and generate the desired hypnotic state; namely, the state of deep trance. And to achieve that goal, repeatedly we used the words dream, go to sleep or relax, prayers organized in small Subliminal created for that purpose; in order, directing the subject to enter the desired hypnotic trance state. And the best way to do this would be as follows: On the count of 3, you ordain you to close your eyes and close your eyes desire you to relax deeply until you start to get that feeling Deep Sleep, I want as you hear my voice, and tell you go to sleep feel a sense of peace and tranquility that makes you get into a deeper and deeper relaxation, as you relax you deeper and deeper feel like you fall into a deep sleep that produces you every more and more desire to sleep, right, so you're doing very well. Perfect, now that you have entered a state of deep relaxation the more you hear my voice, more and more you travel deeper into that deep sleep that gives you serenity and inner peace that you produce that stimulates you to SLEEP DEEPLY more and more. Okay, so, you're doing it correctly. Now I'll start counting from 1 to 3 and as I count going deeper and deeper and deeper into this state of deep relaxation, and I want you perceive as with every breath you relax more and more. That's right, very good; 1 inhales deeply and feel like with every breath you full of tranquility and inner peace that gives you serenity, 2 with every desire exhalation let go of all stress and feel exhale the air from your lungs feel you release all the tensions of your body, 3 feels like more and go deeper and deeper into this state of deep relaxation, right, so you're doing very well. Perfect, now go to sleep soundly. Ready; here if we did induction properly, we have generated in the person desired trance state, now we just have to move on to the next part of induction.

RIGHT GUESS: Should start applying simple suggestions and direct inductions. The successful combination of these suggestions and inductions will allow us to get, we make it much easier to bring the subject (patient or participant) to a state of Trace Hypnotic wanted. If you manage to achieve this disassociation between your conscious and your unconscious mind hypnotic session or show we will have succeeded. And to achieve this, we must follow the previously mentioned steps, as this can create a sequence or continuity in the hypnotic process, and the greater number of successes have greater the chances of success that we get.

YES-SET TECHNIQUE: We must have put the subject (patient or participant) from us. And to achieve this goal we must ensure that the person matches the affirmative and agrees with us at least 3 "YES" followed. For example, you can sit "Yes", you can raise your legs "Yes", you can take a deep breath "Yes". From that moment, it will be much simpler than your subconscious mind accesses our suggestions and inductions more freely, which will carry out the hypnotic session or entertainment show to the next level, activating the desired hypnotic phenomena.

POSITIVE REINFORCEMENT: How does the subject *(Patient or participant) if you are performing at any given time, you are doing it correctly*? It is a question that often tends to go through the mind of the person, either consciously or unconsciously. For this reason, it is vital that the person receiving the suggestions and inductions, know what is happening, happening or done in the process of hypnotic trance, is precisely what has to happen. To do this, continually reinforce the actions of the subject (patient or participant) with positive words and statements such as: "That's very good," "excellent, you're doing great," "right, so you're doing very well". FOR EXAMPLE: If we see that suddenly makes a sudden movement, we will reinforce that action, as if that was normal, "That's great," he feels like that movement makes you enter more and more into a deep trance,

ASSOCIATION: We associate our suggestions and inductions to internal and external experiences of the subject (patient or participant). If for example there any noise outside that is out of our control, then we can use that sound in our favor; suggesting that if "Listen" any outside noise makes focusing more and more on their inner peace - If on the contrary the subject (patient or participant) makes any sudden or involuntary movement such as a slight flicker or arm movement - you can suggest that "feel" with every blink performing or each arm movement allows you to enter more and more into the desired state of hypnotic trance. And thus, we use internal and external situations of the individual, and positively associate the context of our hypnotic session,

METAPHOR USE: Metaphors are figurative and allegorical language that works very well as an excellent persuasive resources in hypnotic communication, which allows us to subconsciously associate a desired state of mind or state of consciousness altered an everyday occurrence, allowing the subject (patient or participant) potentially stimulate SUBJECTIVE alternate reality thus helping to stimulate and develop responses get ideo motor, sensory ideo, and ideo-emotional at an unconscious level and cause activate your alternate reality SUBJECTIVE; and thus, it is much simpler than the subject (patient or participant) receives the [guidance, instruction, suggestions, hypnotic suggestions and direct or indirect inductions] that we are ordering. FOR EXAMPLE:

REPRESENTATION OF SENSORY SYSTEMS: We must adapt to sensory representational system or Sub modalities the subject (patient or participant), whether this is "Visual, is represented by what he sees; Aural represents what listen out; or kinesthetic will represent their emotions, feelings and sensations you feel. " When the group is done HYPNOSIS then we must refer multisensory the three main states that are (sight, hearing, and sensation). Some examples of the items that we can use in our hypnotic sessions or show performances are as follows.

notes as everything that happens around you makes you more and more relaxed.
***Listen out** as everything that happens around you makes you more and more relaxed*
***feels** as everything that happens around you makes you more and more relaxed.*

VERBAL REPRESENTATION or oral communication: The power of the spoken word is our greatest ally; For this reason, our voice, rhythm, cadence, timbre, volume and intonation harmoniously should represent what our spoken word says. FOR EXAMPLE: If we induce or suggestible the subject (patient or participant) to a state of hypnotic sleep, we have to say phrases like: In more and more into a "dream, dream, dream DEEP" "That's very good "" excellent, you're doing great "NOW" fast asleep "

The first induction or suggestion we make a tone volume or low, soft, warm voice whispering; the second, which is the direct hypnotic command we provoke, we pronounced after reinforcement used for interleaving one pray other; but this time with a tone or volume of more loudly and with authority.

However, if we want to induce or suggest him the subject (patient or participant) to enter a state of deep relaxation, we would have to pronounce phrases and sentences composed as follows: From now on, I want you to feel as you relax DEEPLY and you feel more and more relaxed to the extent that you experience an inner peace and RELAX; So, right you're doing fine.

These phrases should then speak tone, rhythm, cadence and intonation of voice that subtly express the state of relaxation and inner peace that we want to lead within your conscious and subconscious mind.

hypnotic voice: As hypnotists PROFESSIONALS, whether we are (street hypnotist, hypnotists show of shows, clinical hypnotists or hypnotherapists specialists) we always make use of two (2) types of voice, our normal voice (which is what we use in our interactions daily) and our hypnotic voice (which is the persuasive voice we use in our sessions or show to induce trance). That way, whenever the subject (patient or participant) listen to our tone Hypnotic VOICE, will be much easier to recognize and subconsciously access the desired state of trance.

<u>Increase Circle of Power and your level of strength or authority level to a higher level (FP)</u>:

Increase Circle of Power and your level of strength or authority level to a higher level (FP) allows you to develop your skills to the next level Hypnotic (my friend to another level).

This allows them to create direct and indirect orders, inductions and suggestions for optimal and effective way, gradually rising in grades HYPNOSIS. That is, they manage to ascend from the circle of power and force level or level of authority to a higher level FP0 and FP1, until FP5 and higher, which enables them to produce certain hypnotic phenomena that would otherwise be impossible.

> *This principle is one of the advanced elements MOST IMPORTANT TO CONSIDER WHEN TO DEEPEN AND INDUCE HYPNOTICS STATES IN GRADES HIGHER OF HYPNOSIS.*
>
> *For this reason, I have written a whole chapter full on this point in particular. Hypnosis is all a masterful art and desire to share you the advanced techniques that are mostly reserved for other books and omitted many of the courses. So later, I will share whatever any (Street hypnotist, hypnotist show of shows, clinical hypnotist or hypnotherapist specialist) shares publicly and openly ... Do you like the idea of learning these advanced techniques, right? Yes. Ok then, without further ado we continue.*

<u>Find your own style and develop it</u>

This element is the most important to keep in mind when you begin to induce and create hypnotic states. My personal experience in the wonderful world of hypnosis, has taught me that to be a good hypnotist or hypnotherapist must first become the hypnotist; ie, feel, think and act like the hypnotist who want to become. Or, in other words, see yourself as the hypnotist, Hypnotist, hypnotist or hypnotherapist who can become. Always keep your attitude, charisma, confidence and security in yourself outweigh any therapeutic script, pre-hypnotic chat, linguistic trick, induction technique, suggestion, hypnotic patterns or commands. Since these are only elements that you will use as a professional to strengthen your presentation;

To start creating your own style, the first thing to do is identify which of the different specialties Hypnotic going to choose to start your way. And these options can be: make yourself known as a hypnotist in events of street hypnosis, or become a hypnotist hypnosis show theater shows; or if you prefer so you can opt for university- be titled and professionally practice as a clinical hypnotist or hypnotherapist specialist. But whatever the decision you make, you should always prepare yourself, take action and make things happen, so that you can be the best in the area you choose.

Another thing you should do to Find your own style and develop it is to choose the type of hypnosis you will use to start your way as a hypnotist, hypnotist or hypnotherapist. Among the different and multiple options exist can specialize in: Hypnosis Classic, Hypnosis Freudian, Hypnosis Show, Hypnosis Clinic, Therapeutic

Hypnosis, hypnosis induction Indirectly Ericksonian Hypnosis, Hypnosis Psycholinguistics, Hypnosis with NLP, Hypnosis Conversational or combination them according to your tastes, preferences, style and personality. And to also combine them according to the situation and occasion demands. Remember the HYPNOSIS offers endless options and unlimited chances, so you take advantage in your favor on your way to personal excellence.

These are just some of the most basic and important to be present at a session of hypnosis clinic or hypnotherapeutic basic principles, as well as in shows of street hypnosis or show. As I said before this book is only a small guide theoretical and practical reference, to introduce you to the wonderful world of hypnosis. It is for this reason I have seen fit to share with you only the most significant and important first steps and basics of hypnosis.

Rules 15 Hypnotic Suggestion:

1. **BRIEF**. Our brain can process data simultaneously five, and even seven, but not ten, or twenty. For this reason, the must avoids building suggestions and long inductions such as: "The heaviness of your arm moves first toward his left foot, then to his right hand, before reaching his forehead, finally returning to his left foot". It is better to say: "The heaviness of her arm, a little bit shifted towards its foot." "The heaviness of her foot, moves very slowly toward his hand," etc. Do you see are the same suggestions and inductions, but declared shorter and accurately?

2. **SPECIFICALLY, and ACCURATE**. He will say: "His arm is getting heavier and heavier as lead," "Your hand every time becomes more and more rigid as a steel rod," "Your eyes are becoming heavier and heavier, her eyelids they close and feel the sensation of entering into a deep sleep. "

3. **AFFIRMATIVE IN THIS TIME**. As if what we said was happening at this time in the here and NOW: "It feels heavy or tired; you feel relaxed or calm. " Better not say, "I would like you to feel heaviness in ..."

4. **POSITIVE**. The suggestion will be accepted much better, the greater the improvement that provides the individual: an example of how it should not be: "We will prevent any disease by quitting smoking." Instead, an example of how SI should be: "Your lungs are cleared, your breathing is energetic, his urge to smoke decrease and you feel more and healthier".

5. **REPEATED**. If a subject is told that his body is heavy directly (your body is heavy, your body is heavy, too heavy ...) it is more likely that we will finally provoke lust. The right thing would be to say as follows: "His body gradually becomes more and more light, your body now begins to feel completely light, becoming lighter and lighter, his legs and hands also It is becoming more and lighter gradually. Each of my words, makes both your body, legs and arms, and feel even lighter. So, light you feel the sensation of levitating, so light that it feels completely relaxed "(As you see we are saying the same thing but differently)

6. <u>**SIMPLE or SUPERIMPOSED**</u>. These two tools, is to relate a fact to another (though in fact have no relationship to each other)

SIMPLE "His arm is becoming lighter and lighter."

SUPERIMPOSED "The lighter your arm becomes, the deeper he sinks into sleep; lighter between his arm becomes more and more relaxes your body and more and more feel a sense of deep sleep. "

This superimposed suggestion, as you may notice makes the relationship a simple suggestion. As you saw in the inductions, there is actually a real relationship between the two; It is the ability of the hypnotist conviction that creates it.

7. <u>**Immediate or delayed**</u>:

DEFERRED "After counting up to three you lift up your left arm."

IMMEDIATE "Raise your left arm now."

Deferred has two advantages: 1 allows preventing the subject, especially regarding physical contact if necessary; and thus, avoid generating some excitement. 2 ° But in itself, used properly, is another hypnotic action that drives the individual to respond before an order and provide another reality ... Through the simple power of their imagination and hyper-suggestibility.

Also, it has two immediate advantages: 1 View the degree of attention and suggestibility of the subject before direct orders. 2nd to assess the level of hypnosis where the subject is. If you respond immediately to the order of "Raise your left arm" means is in the state Z2.

8. <u>**INTRAHIPNÓTICA or posthypnotic**</u>:

INTRAHIPNÓTICA: It occurs during hypnosis. (Ie, are hypnotic phenomena that occur during hypnosis).

posthypnotic: Refers to the time after hypnosis. (That is, are the orders and hypnotic suggestions, which are maintained even after finishing the hypnosis session). For example:

"From now on, whenever you touch the forehead and tell you to sleep, you will enter a state of deep hypnotic trance even more, than you are now. Now, to prove that you understood, accepted and assimilated everything I've told you, I'm going to count to three (3) and wake up. And you will see that you will find you well and you will feel full of energy and vitality; but even after waking up, whenever you touch the forehead and tell you to sleep, you close your eyes and again enter a state of hypnosis further and deeper than you are now, if you understand nods.

ONCE CREATED THE ORDER; and the subject wakes up, test the suggestion posthypnotic, will pass the slight hand and gently across the face (activating the kinesthetic anchor) and tell SLEEPS (activating auditory and sensory anchor) and if the person understood, accept and assimilate all order was implemented was previously re-enter the state of deep hypnotic trance agreed. And ready, we will have already achieved the goal. That's good, right?

---

9. **PROGRESSIVE**. If you tell someone once: "Your relaxed body", you may need to repeat it for fifteen minutes to that feeling really believe in the subconscious of the person. But if you start saying, "Your body starts to relax slowly, feeling like your hands relax more and more, your legs feel like relaxing more and more." "Right, so you're doing very well." "Now you feel peace and tranquility in all your being, feel a sense of well-being throughout your body, now feels that peace, tranquility and feeling of well-being is felt throughout the body and mind, etc." Apprentice, as you can see now we can get the same result as above, but this time, we should only use a maximum of about five minutes and ready.

10. REASONABLE. You always have to anticipate and avoid stressful situations. FOR EXAMPLE: Never shall say, "You are immersed in a deep sleep that covers gradually" to a subject that has been saved from drowning in the sea a few years earlier, as this type of suggestion could cause anxiety. The right thing would be to use INDETERMINATE phrases or unspecific, ie using neutral phrases like: "You slowly relax, feel at peace, calm, your body and your mind begins to feel feelings of well-being, that is, so it is, feels like the feeling of tranquility travels throughout your body, now you feel like you relax more and deeper, feels like the feeling of relaxation allows you to enter gradually into a state of deep sleep, so, right you are doing it very well.

11. FLEXIBLE. In order to adapt to every situation, context or circumstance, as the occasion demands. We must be flexible to adapt our vocabulary and diction at the same dialect word or subject to hypnotize.

12. CONVERGING interrelated. Our suggestions should be consistent with each other, and have a continuous pattern related to the above, to bring the subject finally to the desired hypnotic state. For example: "Your body relaxes, her eyelids weighed and his eyes closed, little heart gradually reduced their rhythm, their breathing slows more and more" is said to converge as each of the suggestions mentioned above stimulate in the subject unconscious memory of the feeling of sleep, leading him to feel the sensation of sleep. As every action mentioned above (representing five natural physiological consequences of sleep) so successfully used this technique, we can artificially create the sensation that occurs in the physiological sleep, using that feeling in our favor.

13.REALIZABLE. If we gave a suggestion that may not be realizable by the subject. Such that (go against their principles, morality, ethics, religion or morals …) In these cases, can happen: 1 Nothing; 2nd The subject wakes up; or 3 ° The subject runs away and takes refuge in the state Z3. For this reason, it is always advisable to give orders, suggestions and inductions that are within their (principles, morality, ethics, religion and morals …) and especially in the correct state Z1 and Z2 and circle of power, strength level or correct level of authority.

14.Reasonable, consistent and coherent. You always have to anticipate physiological reactions. FOR EXAMPLE: We cannot tell the subject that your fingers will begin to separate, when hands are completely open.

15.NORMAL or SUBLIMINAL. A Normal suggestion is meant to be consciously heard by the subject. Lie is a subtle subliminal suggestion and subjectively directed to the subconscious of the person. Normal Suggestions are for example: simple and direct orders, you feel relaxed, your arm levitates, your hands get stuck, your eyes close, your eyelids weigh, etc. While subliminal suggestions are, for example: Invisible images interleaved in a movie, sentences pronounced at high speed or in a tone so low that they cannot hear, or a subtle suggestion or covert order as could be "Every time you hear my voice, you will feel more and more relaxed.

As we could assimilate in this section apprentice, LAS 15 HYPNOTIC SUGGESTION RULES are vital. Learning these 15 principles and adapt them to our sessions of clinical hypnosis therapist or at our shows of street hypnosis show will allow us to be more likely to succeed in our hypnotic's processes.

<u>Work Program to become an excellent HYPNOTIST</u>

1. Preparation of the Voice.

Choose a text, preferably make it interesting and motivating for you; you can use as references suggestibility tests, or hypnotic inductions there in this course; and pronounces each phrase, 4 times in 4 different ways:
- *Paternal authoritarian.*
- *Maternal sweet and affectionate.*
- *Collaborator.*
- *Flexible.*

Here I will share some examples:

Paternal	*Authority.* "*Obedience respect*".	"*Get up immediately!*" *And come here, please.*
Maternal	*Sweetness, Protection.* "*Obedience of love*".	"*I would like you to get up to catch that box: is that I feel very tired.*"
Collaborator	*Analytical Intelligence.* "*Obedience by logical reasoning*".	"*That smoke can be harmful; You should get up and open the window.* "*Do not you think?*
Flexible	*Freedom of Choice, Suggested initiative.* "*Obedience through an apparent freedom of choice.*"	"*Imagine getting up. Cause that desire internally to you; do it when you want and feel you should do it and do it.* "

For this exercise, if necessary, the hypnotist can use these four voices in less than fifteen seconds. This gives an idea of the necessary adaptation.

It should be emphasized at this point, it is not enough just reading these suggestions; You must be aware of the imitation you do when you utter inductions, to seek to accurately pronounce the hypnotic command, through adequate Using a specific voice tone, speaking with a voice that reflects the emotion you want to wake up, describing mental images that create the subject a sense of deepening the state we want to induce.

2. Look in the mirror. Practice the previous exercise, talk to your four Paternal authoritarian voices - Maternal, sweet and loving - *Collaborator Y Flexible*.
For this two-step; looking in the mirror, tries to reflect the following:
THE BREATHING Change the style of ...
- **Rhythm** *"Balanced or uncontrolled " - "Slow or Suave"*
- **Shape** *"Abdominal or Pectoral"*
- **Volume** *"Sufficient or insufficient"*

EYE MOVEMENTS use your eyes in different directions ...
- *Upward, toward the left.*
- *Upwards, towards the right.*
- *Laterally toward the end tip of the left eye.*
- *Laterally to the tip end of the right side of the eye.*
- *Down towards the right.*
- *Down, toward the right*

Written by the **Master Coach YLICH TARAZONA**

MICRO-FACIAL EXPRESSIONS using your face about making gestures ...

- "Gestures" of doubt, fear, fear, anger, restlessness, tension, Relaxation, Excitement, Joy, security, happiness, peace, love and harmony.

BODY POSTURE, Head position and hand movements

- *"Movements of Affirmation" - "Movements of Denial"*
- *"Gestures and movements with the hands and fingers"*
- *"Hard" - "Laid" - "Quiet or Imperative"*

THE VOICE Use your voice in different style ...

- ***Rhythm*** *"Paused or fast"*
- ***Doorbell*** *"High or low"*
- ***Tone*** *"Smooth or Rough"*
- ***Volume*** *"High or low"*

3. Build Suggestions on the basis of a hypnotic state you want to generate.

To carry out this exercise, you can help by applying the sixteen rules of suggestion with which I began this chapter. Learn these sixteen rules. Read text from one of the suggestions you've already created and ask yourself why certain suggestion would not serve sentences.

When talking; analyzes what happens if you say the phrases:
- *Very quickly / slowly*
- *With Tone Neutral / emphatic*
- *Very weak / strong*

4. Learn 5 Steps of a hypnosis session, studying States, Grades and levels of hypnosis, techniques, tools and Families of hypnosis.

States a hypnosis session (Induce, deepen, hypnotic phenomena, post-hypnotic suggestion and process of awakening); States and levels of hypnosis (STATUS MONITOR "Z0" - Present here and now, neuronal level BETA = between 14 to 28 Hz or (cycles per second or cps) - STATE HIPNOIDAL or Charm Z0 and Z1, neuronal level ALPHA / ALPHA = 8 to 13 Hz or (cycles per second or fps) - TRANCE HYPNOTIC SLIGHT or Superficial Z1, neuronal level ZETA / THETA = 4 to 7 Hz or (cycles per second or fps) - TRANCE HYPNOTIC MEDIUM or cataleptic Z1 and Z2 , neuronal level ZETA / THETA = 4 to 7 Hz or (cycles per second) - HYPNOTIC TRANCE THRESHOLD somnambulic or somnambulism Z2, neuronal level DELTA = 0,5 3 Hz or (cycles per second or cps), outwardly perceptible) ; Magnetism technique (MOPPAO); Tools Mesmer (Fascination and suggestion); Family Hypnosis (Sensorial, physiological, Psicoimaginaria, Psicoconflictiva); Purpose, strategy and phraseology of the families of hypnosis.

5. Learn the Purpose, Strategy and phraseology of sensory FAMILIES, Physiological, Psicoconflictiva And Psicoimaginaria. Apprentice, for this exercise have to be able to adapt the 4 families of hypnosis to all cases. You know what each one, understand its stages and the corresponding order of each objective, strategy and phraseology.

6. Invent New Techniques Suggestions. In this exercise, the purpose is to design, create and innovate new suggestions and hypnotic from 4 families of hypnosis (sensory, physiological, Psicoconflictiva and Psicoimaginaria) using new already known and studied in this course of hypnosis techniques, or inductions. The important thing is to do it in writing and based on:

a) Purpose.
b) Strategy and
c) phraseology

7. Mastering various techniques of suggestion, and what guidance is appropriately chosen the most suitable rare each induction, depending on the situation, context and circumstances that arise.

Most hypnotists:

- Begin with a previous interview, a pre-hypnotic, talk write their medical report, they read and fill the therapeutic script with the patient or participant, fill the contract or posthypnotic agreement to keep in mind the goals they want to achieve with the session or show, deepening the reason for the consultation or session, ask questions on the subject to locate possible psychological and physiological problems, if any, detect fears, traumas, phobias, expectations, desires and interests, etc.

- Use the test of suggestibility fall back (Family Sensory) and reliable test methods to check the degree of suggestibility of the subject. To achieve better results, it is recommended (Go changing the tone, volume, tempo and rhythm of the voice to find out which works best in that subject and adapt to each situation or context in particular) - "If the subject put some resistance, subtly you switched style voice, auditory perception, visual, kinesthetic and sensory be incorporated to stimulate the desired hypnotic state the person, and finally to achieve the goal; it begins with the deepening of using other technical or family.)

> **IMPORTANT NOTE** Some of these elements, principles, strategies, phraseology, families and sensory tools hypnotist ... We will see and study further in the second book of this series: book entitled "HYPNOSIS COURSE PRACTICE - *How to hypnotize, anyone, Anytime, Anywhere ©-® "*.
>
> *So, champions and champions, this book is just the beginning of what you learn in the entire series, to prepare for you, and which is made in 3 volumes ...*
>
> *So, with this in mind, let's continue ...*

Good **LEARNERS**, we have **reached the end of this fourth chapter**! I hope you enjoyed it and especially you've learned a lot about **Start Blocks for use hypnosis**. As always apprentice, I wish you luck with your education. Mastery of all these theoretical concepts hypnosis, your learning is important because they are the pillars that allow you to take your hypnotic capabilities to the next level. Remember that *(You can always count on me for anything you need) Keep in mind that "If you have any questions, you can "write directly to me (E-mail)".*

Well, I hope to read your messages from the "Comments" section of my website! Ah! APPRENTICE, I would also like you to comment me lessons or experiences you have had with reading this book. Until next time my dear reader- I hope to have news soon yours ... ^ _ ^!

MásterCoach.YlichTarazona@gmail.com
http://www.reingenieriamentalconpnl.com

SUCCESS IS FOR THOSE THAT WE ARE WILLING TO PAY THE PRICE AND ENJOY THE ROAD
"Success is more than one condition is a state of mind. Success is a journey; It is the consecutive achievement of small goals, and is the result of a life with purpose. And so, our goals are carried out; We must be willing to set our minds toward our destination, take action, implement the plan or project life and make things happen.
-. YLICH TARAZONA. -

CHAPTER V: DIFFERENCES AND FUNCTIONS OF THE CONSCIOUS MIND, THE CRITICAL FACTOR, THE SUBCONSCIOUS MIND AND THE UNCONSCIOUS

Well champions and champions once studied and understood the history of hypnosis, the suggestions with persuasive patterns and their evolution through history and its multiple functions and applicability in different contexts and therapeutic hypnosis shows. Now let's focus on a subject that is essential and fundamental to understand to understand the hypnotic phenomena we have been discussing in earlier chapters. And these concepts are the conscious and the subconscious mind; terms that we have already mentioned above, and we will use as the basis of study to understand the hypnotic processes described throughout the book.

Although many studies on the subject, so far has never been identified in the brain, which is the actual source where the human mind resides. While it is true; which, in most cases, the term MIND is used as a reference to an object. As indicated, and appropriate to refer to the serious mind as a function or brain process.

In some way; MIND expression refers to the actions and interactions between cells, neurons, synapses and electrochemical processes occurring in our brain. In another order of ideas; MIND terminology is used to describe all cognitive activities of the brain, thought processes, information processing and various multisensory stimuli from the outside world perceived by our 5 senses (VA- K- "O and G") Visual, auditory, kinesthetic or sensory impairment.

It is for this reason that, in hypnosis, suggestion and Persuasive PATTERNS study brain function and cerebral hemispheres, as well as the mind and conscious components, subconscious, unconscious and critical, are essential for understanding wonderful world of Hypnosis and Persuasion.

Although there are four (4) components of the human mind (conscious, subconscious, unconscious and critical) Among the most important processes in which we will focus our attention on this part of the book; are brain processes occurring within our "{(CONSCIOUS MIND)}" and our "{(subconscious mind)}".

The Conscious Mind:

also known as logical mind, thinking or rational mind. It is the program analyzes, codifies and simplifies the information we receive in the alert status or state of watch. For that reason; the conscious mind plays the role of judge by the critical factor in the workings of the brain. The conscious mind is what allows us to evaluate the importance of the information that reaches us through different sensory stimuli (sight, hearing, touch, smell and taste). Allowing us to either accept or reject the hypnotic inductions and suggestions persuasive or used appropriately in the hypnosis sessions patterns.

It is estimated that the conscious mind, allegorically speaking displayed figuratively as the tip or top of a large iceberg, only constitutes from 1% to 10% percent of our total brain capacities, ie our mind.

One of the most important activities of the conscious mind is to allow through hypnosis or self-hypnosis BioProgramar our subconscious mind. And this mental programming occurs; when we focus and focus our thoughts on inductions or suggestions, and accept or internalize consciously and voluntarily as if it were an unquestionable truth, bringing the effect of creating a new reality and as a result generate new neural connections associated with programming recently incorporated into our brains.

Subconscious Mind:

Known mostly as intuitive or instinctive mind. Using the analogy of a computer the subconscious mind would become the hard drive or internal memory center where we installed our programs and mental maps, being therefore the suggestible or BioProgramable part of our brain.

It is estimated that the subconscious mind, allegorically represented, is as deep or internal mass or inside of a large iceberg, which constitutes 90% to 95% percent of our total brain capacities, ie our mind. This is where they take live our beliefs, values and mental maps.

Other major tasks of our subconscious mind are to record, save, record, encode and remember the information reaching our brain through our senses. As well as accept the suggestions, commands or hypnotic patterns induced by hypnosis.

It is for this reason that in the states of TRANCES HYPNOTICS is stimulated in the subject (patient or participant) the "hyper - suggestibility". That is, the ability to receive and accept orders or suggestions we suggest you through inductions.

Through the correct hypnotic suggestion, we amplify the multi-sensory responses subject (patient or participant) and deepen the evocative experiences; I helping develop responses ideo motor, sensory ideo, and ideo-emotional that allows them to experience individual's personal transformations of a much more efficiently, effectively and more permanently, if you perform the same hypnotic procedure in alertness or wakeful state. Because it is from the subconscious mind where different hypnotic phenomena occur.

Unconscious Mind on the other hand, is responsible for controlling a variety of the most automated processes governing the functioning of our body. Such as heart rate, circulation, our breath; as well as the proper functioning of the internal systems of the body that are vital to human life.

Therefore, it is hoped that the unconscious mind and subconscious mind work together, and always keep awake and be alert to control each and every one of those automatic body processes. Functions and processes that continue to function even when we sleep or enter states of relaxation, meditation or DEEP HYPNOTIC TRANCE.

The unconscious mind likewise, is associated as the epicenter where the body's hormone levels are regulated and your survival instincts are generated and your intuitive sense either fight or flight facing a dangerous situation. And all this happens unconsciously and instinctively without thinking consciously put yourself in the unexpected event that arose from unintended way. All these internal changes immediately occur automatically, without even realize we know of them. In this sense, we could say that this automatic process that occurs within us, is one of the great powers governing the unconscious mind.

As a recap: The normal functions of the unconscious and the subconscious mind, we could define in these 3 processes ...

The physical side: It has to do with the regular and essential processes for the preservation of life and the restoration of welfare that includes an instinctive desire for overall survival.

The mental side It is the storehouse of memory; cherishes the wonderful messages of thought, working free of time and space; It is the source of the practical initiative and constructive forces that shape our habits and create our mental programming, maps, beliefs and values.

The spiritual side Is the source of ideals, aspirations, desires, imagination, and is the means through which we recognize our connection to the Divine Source we call God. And in proportion as we recognize this connection we come to a greater understanding of our divine nature.

<u>Critical Factor</u> Between the conscious mind and the subconscious mind, there unconscious process called the "critical factor". The (FC) is not a physical or tangible part of the brain; but rather, it is a function or allegorical or metaphorical concept of how the mind works. The (FC) is the part of the mind that decides to accept or not accept as truth. Note I do not say that "accepts the truth" if no "truth" and that every human mind interprets the truth subjectively. That is, that every truth is different for each person and the interpretation of it is that creates such a reality. In other words, the critical factor is the "gatekeeper" between the conscious and the subconscious that creates the reality of the individual.

<u>Sketch of the human mind</u>

- ✓ CONSCIOUS MIND
- ✓ CRITICAL FACTOR
- ✓ Subconscious Mind
- ✓ UNCONSCIOUS PROCESS

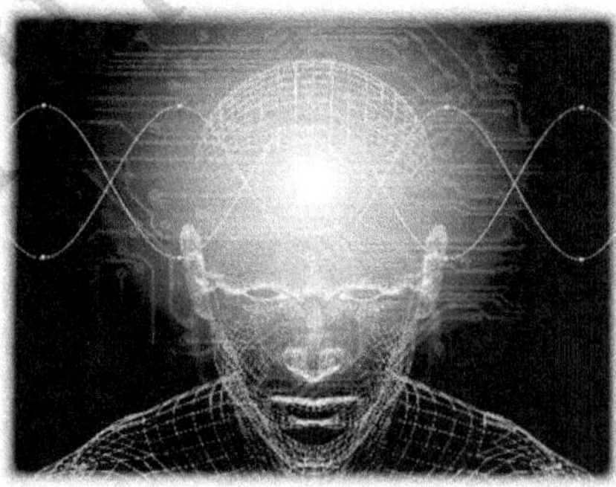

<u>PROCESSES AND FUNCTIONS OF THE MIND</u>

<u>THE UNCONSCIOUS:</u>
The unconscious is the Wisdom of the Body.
   ✓ It is the first part of the mind that develops in the early stages of pregnancy, when the formation of life of the baby in the womb of the mother begins.

   ✓ The unconscious mind records all the information we receive in the beginning; first through electro-chemical reactions. That is, that at the time they conceived; the unconscious mind records all loads multisensory messages we receive. First of [energy way] through the thoughts, feelings and emotions that are manifestations of energy in the body, which are presented in the form of electrical and chemical reactions (electrochemical) that spread throughout the body, through a [intraorgánico] language and the brain; in training, recorded in your unconscious mind, without having the opportunity of rejecting or accepting. As a result of this act; Unconscious begins to form, he begins to perceive clearly, but linguistic understanding impressions of what happens inside and outside their environment. And so, begins to [cause] the unconscious mind; as it begins to perceive certain feelings and emotions, now learns to recognize [psychologically] and that, indeed, this will be part of her unconscious registration. These being the first [origins] of our first mental programming.

✓ The unconscious mind intuitively knows all activities of the human body; and the proper functioning of our organs and systems, such as heartbeat, circulation, breathing, sweating, *expansion or contraction of muscles growth (bones, teeth, nails, hair); as well as controls and regulates the functioning of the digestive, kidney, liver processes including hormonal functions. The unconscious mind also controls the immune system or the body's defense system; and for that reason, it is responsible for the self-regeneration of the body, being responsible to heal and heal our bodies.*

✓ The unconscious mind controls secretions of various hormones produced in the human body; among some of them they are:

- *Adrenalin "In charge of risk situations"*
- *serotonin "The charge of boost morale"*
- *Insulin "Responsible for regulating glucose.*
- *dopamine "Hormone Welfare"*
- *melatonin "Hormone Dream"*
- *Exotocina "Love Hormone"*
- *cortisol "Stress Hormone"*

✓ The unconscious mind and responsible for the automatic or programmed behavior, such as: the preservation of species *and mating*

✓ The unconscious mind controls basic survival instincts; such as: Eat, swallow, suck, sucking, nurse, etc.

✓ UNCONSCIOUS MIND *It is designed to handle survival from a binary system: Run away or **Fight** Admit or repel.*

✓ The unconscious mind is programmed to respond or react subjectively to feelings of pleasure and pain: Humans inevitably closer look and identify more with those sensory stimuli that us pleasure. *For this reason, it is much simpler than people respond more positively to suggestions and inductions associated with enjoyment, acceptance and pleasure, instead of multi-sensory sensations that cause situations of flight, fear or pain. In other words, the human being is programmed to respond or react subjectively almost to two (2) possible stimuli or hypnotic responses, which are:*

1 And suggest us approach to rewards us pleasure.

2nd Away to avoid or evade the consequences that cause us pain.

✓ The unconscious mind is related to our feelings; While Sean joy, sadness, grief, anger, rage, guilt, happiness, depression, enthusiasm. That is, the unconscious mind has the ability to experience emotions and express feelings through physical and physiological expressions.

✓ The unconscious mind is related to autoimmune diseases and psychosomatic problems. Symptoms somatize physically; causing an illness without numbers. As well as activation response Psychosomatic expressions sometimes caused by emotional problems.

✓ The unconscious mind plays a protective role. That is the ability to protect against infections, external agents, foreign pathogens bacteria and microorganisms. And it is also responsible for our reflexes and instincts of survival.

✓ The unconscious mind is related to the reptilian brain and brain stem, which are the first to form in the evolutionary scale.

Subconscious mind:
The subconscious mind is the database or hard disk.

✓ The subconscious mind is where all information multisensory contact humans through 5 senses (sight, hearing, touch, smell and taste) is recorded.

✓ Subconscious mind begins empty; and it is filled with information in the course of our entire life.

✓ In the subconscious mind is recorded multisensory form everything we see, hear, we feel, smell and tasted.

✓ Subconscious Mind

✓ Information from the subconscious mind is recorded and recorded in our brains, creating what we call GROOVE NEURONAL or connections NEURAL these being the cause of our mental programming, habits, behaviors and behaviors before certain events, situations and life events.

✓ The subconscious mind is responsible for the permanent short MEMORY, medium or long term.

✓ The subconscious mind records everything with which we come into contact, like a recorder that records, logs and operates 24 hours a day and night. And it has the capacity to store more than 2500 years of data, ie more than ten quintillion of bytes of information. Can you imagine THE POWER OF THE HUMAN MIND? so far nothing has been able to overcome, not even match the powers that underlie our brain and in the depths of the subconscious mind.

✓ The subconscious mind is responsible for our lifelong learning. That is, the subconscious mind continues to learn and record new information constantly every day, every day, until the end of our days

✓ The subconscious mind is ANALOGUE, encodes and processes information simultaneously.

✓ The subconscious mind is the database or hard drive of the human mind and has the ability to record:

- ***Experiences*** *People, situations and events.*
- ***Thoughts*** *Positives: Negatives + or -.*
- ***Emotions*** *Fear-Courage, Joy-Sadness, Depression-Happiness.*
- ***Memories****: Royals Created induced, altered or distorted.*

✓ The subconscious mind is unlimited and infinite. And working together, holistic, comprehensive and synergistic with the unconscious; and uses 95 to 98% of our brain capacity.

✓ The subconscious mind shapes our personality and behavior through a set of:

• ***Emotions***, *Experiences, memories, and learning paradigms (maps of reality) that enhance, create and modify our neural grooves or neural connections that eventually become our mental programming, habits and beliefs that are fixed and installed in our brain.*

✓ The subconscious mind can be either, responsible for intuition or Need for Change; or resistance or fear of change.

✓ The subconscious mind meets the protective function of keeping all information recorded conscious and stable. thus, avoiding any sudden change in our personality no apparent reason.

✓ The subconscious mind stimulates our emotions to meet needs. And it is responsible for BioProgramar or reprogram the necessary changes, and the creation or modification of neural connections when the occasion requires it. *And it can be reprogrammed BioProgramadas or consciously and unconsciously, induced or self-induced.*

✓ Subconscious mind relates to the limbic system or mammalian brain, which is the second form in the developmental stage, directly related to the hypothalamus.

THE CONSCIOUS MIND:
The conscious mind is what is present here and now.

✓ The conscious mind is responsible for rational thinking, logical and analytical functions related to intellectual processes.

✓ The conscious mind is responsible for Willpower.

• *Is the force or energy that motivates us and drives us to start making changes or stay in the same state.*

• *Force or energy is driven by our emotions, thoughts and actions.*

• *It is the force or energy that increases or decreases according to our emotional, mental and emotional states so it tends to be very volatile, uncertain and hesitant at times.*

✓ The conscious mind is responsible to anticipate, plan, act, perform, develop, monitor, assess and make decisions.

✓ The conscious mind is LIMITED represents only 2 to 5% approximately brain capacity *(Only the tip of Iceberg).*

✓ The conscious mind works with the cerebral hemispheres *(Left hemisphere and right hemisphere of the brain)*

✓ The conscious mind processes an average of only a 7 to 9 bit of information, which makes limited in certain situations and circumstances.

✓ The conscious mind is related to consciousness, language and conscious and voluntary physical processes.

✓ The conscious mind meets the protective function to protect us from the immediate dangers perceived by the 5 senses.

✓ The conscious mind is responsible for creating our immediate possible reality.

✓ The conscious mind is related to the neocortex brain or cerebral cortex, which is the last to appear and evolve on the evolutionary scale.

CRITICAL FACTOR or Critical Factor of Mind
The critical factor is the guardian of mind.

✓ The critical factor is the comparison mechanism of the mind.

- *Critical Factor compares the new information in your immediate present, with all the log information stored in your subconscious mind and determine what should or should not enter and be programmed or decoded from your conscious mind.*

✓ The critical factor is the guardian of the mind and brain function that determines what to accept or reject the information it receives from its environment and the environment through the 5 senses.

✓ The critical factor functions as a filter that evaluates the new information recorded through multisensory channels, in order to allow or reject the storage of new information processed in our subconscious mind.

✓ CRITICAL FACTOR compares and evaluates new incoming information and links it with the information and analyzes that already has recorded and stored. If it makes sense accepts it, or else, it makes sense he rejects it as a means of prevention and survival. And this makes a mental, psychological, emotional and physical level unconsciously.

✓ The critical factor is a mechanism for continuous and ongoing comparison and evaluation between the information recorded in the unconscious mind and the subconscious mind with the newly recorded information stored and entered by the conscious mind.

✓ The critical factor is to PROTECTOR safeguard and protect the information stored in the depths of the unconscious mind and the subconscious mind function.

CHAPTER VI: CIRCLE POWER LEVEL POWER LEVEL OF AUTHORITY OR HIGHER LEVEL (FP)

Hello my dear readers such, we have reached one of the most important to learn to master hypnosis as some professional chapters. And it's increase Circle of Power and your level of Force Majeure or level of authority to a higher level (FP). These techniques and advanced knowledge will allow you to develop your hypnotic skills to the next level.

This means that this knowledge and advanced techniques allow you to create direct and indirect orders, subjective inductions and effective suggestions for optimal and effectively in the ascending scale levels of hypnosis. gradually rising in grades HYPNOSIS ELDERLY; getting up from a circle POWER or lower force level to a higher level of authority or intermediate and higher level of hypnosis. Allowing you to literally gradually ascending from an FP0, FP1, FP2, until FP5, FP6, FP7 and above. What it entitles you to generate certain hypnotic phenomena that would otherwise be impossible cause, without prior knowledge of these advanced techniques.

This principle is one of the advanced elements most important to consider when Deepen and INDUCE HYPNOTICS STATES IN HIGHER degrees or levels of hypnosis. For this reason, I have written a complete whole chapter on this particular point, so without further ado let's begin.

In the practice of hypnosis, it has been found that each order is given to the subject (patient or participant) is the cumulative force of all inductions and earlier suggestions that have been given. This cumulative process of suggestions, inductions, direct and indirect orders, hypnotic patterns and covert commandos increase Circle of Power and your level of strength to a higher level of authority; ie a level or degree SUPERIOR most advanced hypnosis that will allow you to develop your hypnotic abilities more powerfully; whether they are in your sessions of therapeutic hypnosis or hypnosis shows your shows.

Now to continue and go deeper into this subject; the first thing I'm going to explain are the different degrees or levels of hypnosis. Grade Levels or hypnotics are known as "FP". Mastering the "FP" is allowing you to move up in your CIRCLE OF POWER or your level of strength to a higher level of authority. That is, a higher in degrees or levels of HYPNOSIS LEVEL. In other words, the "FP" is the influence you have and exert persuasive power that in actual practice, when generating orders, suggestions and hypnotic inductions.

LEVELS OF GRADES or HYPNOSIS

FP0.- It is the first degree or level of hypnosis, ie is the suggestible state in which we are at all times. You can say it is the waking state in which we are alert to any information that comes to us through the 5 senses, and we are so consciously attentive to accept or not an idea, opinion or suggestion we receive in our environment.

FP1.- The degree or level FP1 when we started our communication process; that is, when we started subtly convey our ideas in our conversations, opinions or suggestions, so that people with whom we come in contact begin to accept them consciously. I'll give you two (2) Examples: 1 is the most common "FP"; is the "FP1" we use every day in our conversations, allowing us to communicate our ideas, thoughts, feelings, opinions or suggestions to people or individuals with whom we come into contact and interact daily, whether these friends, acquaintances, family and even strangers. And this happens so often and unconsciously, when asked when such a complete stranger and it responds kindly, when we suggest a movie to a good friend and this access to see her happy, when we share a close a thought or a feeling and we are heard, and finally when we share an idea in a group, in our work or study center and this is received and accepted by all IDEA THE TRUTH Do you understand? That is, the "FP1" is the level or degree of hypnosis in which we influence; and which at the same time we are influenced in our daily interactions and conversations with others. - In the 2nd example, the "FP1" applies to hypnosis as such. For example, when we started our hypnotic process with a subject (patient or participant) and started to reach a level of force or positive influence on the person; so that the subject with whom we are interacting starts accessing our suggestions, allowing us to begin to give basic commands and this begins to accept our suggestions and let go voluntarily and knowingly by the inductions we give them. At this point, you can order the (patient or participant) to close his eyes, and this will. You can suggest your eyelids begin to be more and more tired and heavy; and that as deeply relaxes, and is carried away by this feeling of being his eyes began to blink more and more frequently until you feel the desire and the need to close them completely. And once they closed his eyes are so relaxed, you cannot open them. At this point, if the subject followed our instructions correctly, the person can try to open eyes, but cannot do so, since it has accepted the suggestion that they are so relaxed and stuck to them becomes normal unable to open his eyes, allowing you to dive deeper and deeper into the hypnotic state desired "FP1" and opens to be introduced to a force level to a higher level of authority. That is, to a higher level of "FP2" Now you understand the idea, right? This is what is known as CIRCLE OF POWER "FP". That is, this is the first degree or hypnotic level, the "FP1". At a higher level of "FP2" Now you understand the idea, right? This is what is known as CIRCLE OF POWER "FP". That is, this is the first degree or hypnotic level, the "FP1". At a higher level of "FP2" Now you understand the idea, right? This is what is known as CIRCLE OF POWER "FP". That is, this is the first degree or hypnotic level, the "FP1".

FP2.- The "FP2" is when you reach a level or degree of force to a level greater authority in hypnosis. That is, you increase your CIRCLE OF POWER or higher level of influence and persuasion on the subject, so you can instruct your subconscious mind to start moving one finger or one hand levitate. And the person in question; You can start feeling as the case or order received, either begin to feel the trembling of one of his fingers, or literally feel begins to float one hand unconsciously, only through the power of your mind Subconscious and its ability to imagine and recreate the situation that we ordered.

So this degree or level of influence and persuasion exerted on the subject, you can tell or order something like: I want you begin to notice as one of "Your fingers start to move" or a "Your hand starts to levitate "you'll notice as one of" Your fingers begin to tremble "or a" Your hands start to float "and literally if the person in question has followed our instructions previously; and has agreed to follow our orders before, it is more likely that the finger of the subject began to cause a slight tingling sensation and feel begins to move the finger, or in the case of levitation arm, began slowly feel my arm obeys to the degree to lift all alone with the power of your subconscious mind and his ability to imagine and recreate the situation.

To that extent its level of hyper-suggestibility, this obeys and fulfills the order received and make that subjective reality; so that, even if the subject would not move a finger or lower the arm you can no longer do, because he has already accepted the order and your mind subconsciously produced the expected effect. Which it is something that impresses greatly subjects (patients or participants) because are experiencing REAL PHENOMENON HYPNOTIC allowing you to have more control over your subconscious mind; ie it is allowing them to take greater control over himself, realizing the extent of the established order; and experience the desired "FP2" hypnotic state. This opens the door to a force level to a higher level of authority. That is to say, at a higher level of "FP3" Did you see how interesting and powerful is to understand these concepts and apply them correctly? This my friends, is what we know as CIRCLE OF POWER "FP". That is, this is the second degree or hypnotic level, "FP2".

FP3.- To continue with the above idea, we can say conclusively that the "FP3" is a level or degree of superior force of a higher level of authority than the previous "FP2". That is, the "FP3" significantly increases the circle of power, or higher level of influence and persuasion on the subject and so on You see what I mean? That as you move up in grade or level of "FP" your power of influence and persuasion exerted on the subject is also increasing, you hear well what I'm saying? By increasing your "FP" HYPNOTIC also increase your power.

FP3, FP4, FP5.- From the degrees or levels of HYPNOSIS "FP3" "FP4" "FP5" begin to produce the greatest hypnotic phenomena. That is, in these degrees or levels of HYPNOSIS "FP3", "PF4" "FP5" is where it begins to exert greater control over the subconscious mind of the subject, and the phenomena of hypnotic trance MILD or surface Z1 occur, the HYPNOTIC TRANCE MEDIUM or cataleptic Z1-Z2 and HYPNOTIC TRANCE THRESHOLD or somnambulistic Z2. Thus, the subconscious mind of the subject begins to more easily follow orders, instructions, suggestions and inductions that gives the hypnotist.

And it is from here, my dear readers, where the real persuasive resources begin to occur in hypnotic communication. Since these **DEGREES** *or levels of* HYPNOSIS "FP3", "PF4" "FP5" are who allow us to subconsciously associate a desired state of mind or state of consciousness altered an everyday occurrence, allowing the subject (patient or participant) potentially stimulate AC subjective reality helping in this way, to get answers to stimulate and develop ideo motor, ideo sensory, emotional and ideo-top at an unconscious level and cause activate your alternate reality SUBJECTIVE; and thus, it is much more receptive power of the subject (patient or participant) to receive the [guidance, instruction, suggestions, hypnotic suggestions, inductions and direct or indirect orders] that we are establishing.

These degrees or levels of HYPNOSIS "FP3" "FP4" "FP5" are hypnotics processes, which are closely related to certain advanced techniques inductions and verbal suggestions strategically used by specialists, whether clinical hypnotists (hypnotherapists) or hypnotists show theater (street hypnotists), to cause certain hypnotic phenomena of higher level in the individual. As the attention of the subject (patient or participant) focuses on the power of the spoken word of the hypnotist; This eventually through verbal suggestions and hypnotic inductions is superimposed to the inner voice of the subject involved, helping to develop responses of "hyper-suggestibility", "hyper-creativity", "hyper-imagination" "hyper concentration" and "hyper-relaxation".

FP5, FP6, FP7.- (also called "HYPNOTICS Staffs") since they are considered in hypnosis as one of the degrees or higher or higher of achievable levels. These degrees or levels of "FP" has managed to achieve mastery over the body and mind of the subject. And here, my dear readers where we are empowered to order the subject of a clucking like a chicken if you wanted so; and the person comply with the order without objection What interesting way? - Although logically; of course, these levels or degrees also have many other more practical and interesting applications. SUCH AS: Tibetan and Buddhist monks; use this power, degrees or levels of HYPNOSIS "FP5", "FP6" and "FP7" to give the order to walk from one city to another without getting tired. And so, their bodies go into "automatic" walking while their minds may be dreaming, thinking, or thinking about anything else. And so, their bodies arrive in perfect condition to your destination much faster than as they normally would; and also, they do without fatigue or physical fatigue, since in these states, the body remains in a total parasympathetic dominance. That is, in a "state of hyper concentration" (WAVES ALPHA / ALPHA = 8 to 13 Hz, cycles per second or cps) and a "state of rest" and "hyper-relaxation" (WAVES ZETA / THETA = 4 to 7 Hz, cycles per second or cps). Now do you understand the power you have in your hands, learning to master these degrees or levels of HYPNOSIS "FP5", "FP6" and "FP7"?

These degrees or levels of HYPNOSIS "FP5", "FP6" and "FP7" are ideal also to enable lucid dreaming, astral travel or try making body experiences; since these HYPNOTICS STATES or altered states of consciousness, the mind has more control over the physical and etheric body; in a way, much more transcendental, which as you would consciously in the state ALERT or wakeful state.

FP8, FP9, FP10.- (also called "HYPNOTICS STATES HIGH-LEVEL"). The following degrees or levels of HYPNOSIS "FP8", "FP9" "FP10" are what ALTERED STATES of consciousness in Schools Hypnosis is considered "impossible." Theories of degrees or levels of HYPNOSIS "FP8", "FP9" "FP10" believes and states that the hypnotic state is a real state different from the normal state monitors, unique, separately. For this reason, these hypnotic states, degrees or levels of hypnosis "FP8", "FP9" "FP10" can be created and artificially produced by the correct process of hypnotic induction, which alters the subjective experience and phenomenology of the person concerned.

This theory states that and reverberant CIRCLE OF POWER and levels of Force Majeure to an Authority Level or higher (FP) will allow the specialist (street hypnotist, hypnotist show, clinical hypnotist or hypnotherapist) to develop their hypnotic skills to the next level; thus, limiting the critical factor in the mind of the subject (patient or participant) and altering the individual mindfulness through the suggestions and inductions that are offered up and progressively.

This theory of hypnosis levels "FP8", "FP9" "FP10" also states that there are multiple cognitive systems normally work synergistically and holistic under primary control. And, during hypnosis, normally integrated with each other, subsystems are dissociated from one another at different scales and are capable of simultaneous and independent multiple degrees of altered consciousness responses to orders, suggestions and inductions declared by the hypnotist.

<u>DEGREES AND LEVELS OF HYPNOSIS "continuation"</u>

Well my dear readers as we have learned in the previous sections, as specialist (street hypnotist, hypnotist show clinical hypnotist or hypnotherapist) increase our circle of power, or Strength level to a higher level of authority or higher level of HYPNOSIS. We empower ourselves we literally; to go climbing or gradually rising from the FP0, FP1, FP2 levels until grades FP5, FP6, FP7 and above. This will allow us to generate certain hypnotic phenomena that are otherwise impossible cause, without prior knowledge of these advanced techniques.

That is to say; champions and champions, following the idea of the preceding paragraphs. One more specialist who is in some specialties or disciplines of hypnosis, either (street hypnotist, hypnotist show clinical hypnotist or hypnotherapist), we could get a person in the middle of the street at random, and then order him directly to be put to cluck like a chicken or send to deeply relax and sleep ... because this person probably will not! True?...

However, if the subject, either a (participant or patient) is willing to cooperate voluntarily with us in a show of hypnosis show or in a clinical hypnosis session; and you as a hypnotist, have previously followed all the above steps I've taught you, and have gradually increased Circle of Power or Strength Level to a higher level of authority at higher levels of hypnosis. It is more likely at the time that the subject in question (participant or patient), if it has shown its willingness to follow your [guidance, instruction, orders and suggestions] and you have successfully taken by the appropriate pre-hypnotic process; then, is there, at that moment my friend, that if you send them to do something simple, such as CLOSE YOUR EYES, breathing (inhale or exhale deeply) and then invite you to relax and deepen that experience, I assure you it will. Once we have achieved this first step, by earning their trust, and find ourselves as other small [hypnotic suggestions and indirect inductions] very subtle accepted gradually. The subconscious mind of the subject (participant or patient) then began to be more willing to receive our orders growing. And if at that moment we order in a very subtle way but straight to cackle like a hen that person if that will do it? Of course, it will; and the reasons why you will, is because more small order, and after accepting the above suggestions, unconsciously predisposed to accept orders greater intensity.

And if then, to continue the previous idea. Would you suggest another simple induction, then another, then another too small and simple? When you've done several of these inductions; and you've reached a good level of strength, and a good level of authority Mayor favorably. You can order you start to feel like your arm starts to levitate, and gradually feel increasingly like his arm begins to lift, gently float and levitate; Only then, his arm began to rise, float and levitate. Because already it predisposed to follow your instructions, allowing you to enter a state of hyper-suggestibility entitling him to experience these hypnotic phenomena inducing them. And then if you keep giving direct orders, subjective suggestions and inductions more or less the same level, they will fulfill each as part of a whole. And if, then, and the subject (patient or participant) is completely open to your inductions and suggestions, and tell you relax deeply and then you give the order to sleep and tell them with a subtle voice, but with authority Then that person go to sleep, if you are in the desired hypnotic state, the order is accepted by your subconscious mind, so it will! And it will fulfill your order Do you understand? the order is accepted by your subconscious mind, so it will! And it will fulfill your order Do you understand? the order is accepted by your subconscious mind, so it will! And it will fulfill your order Do you understand?

There you have all the "secret" of hypnosis. - FIRST you make the person to relax, you focus on breathing (inhalation and exhalation) and between the alpha state. Then you begin to give simple commands. At first through small inductions, but then you're making these suggestions are getting bigger. Finally, when the subject (patient or participant) delves into the hypnotic experience that you are living, you start giving orders, inductions and suggestions of a level of strength and a higher level of authority; because, your subconscious mind is ready and open to obey, so it will. You realize?

Good champions and champions is that these orders or inductions do not necessarily have to be "direct" suggestions. Since orders, inductions and "small" suggestions can be as simple and easy to perform or continue as telling the subject to "Hearing my voice, part of your body will start to relax right now, the more things and more you concentrate on my voice, more and more you begin to feel and enjoy this state of deep relaxation, and more and more pleasant and relaxed you feel, and more and more enjoy the experience, so much so that relaxation will make you feel very nice and enter a state of hypnosis more and deeper now "have you noticed?

ONE OF THE KEYS TO ALWAYS HAVE TO HAVE THIS IS WHAT: When a person enters states *(WAVES ALPHA / ALPHA STATE = 8 to 13 Hz, cycles per second or cps)* your body begins to relax alone. Thus, you are taking this into account; You can tell the subject in question certainly that: "As you listen to your voice, a part of your body will start to relax now," and sure there's some part of your body that has already begun to relax or and it is relaxing. So intuitively your subconscious is that part of your body that is relaxed or is relaxing; and as the subconscious is very literal (CREE that you are relaxing by the "Order of the hypnotist"). And poufs the hypnotic phenomenon begins to occur. Then when you suggest the following order "I command that relaxation is becoming more and more pleasant and enjoyable," then the subconscious (Listen to your order, notes that is producing your prediction and feels like every time you feel more and more relaxed; and that relaxation is becoming more and more pleasant and enjoyable) and Pleasurable Of course it is! Relaxation Everyone is welcome! But the subconscious does not know, and most importantly NEVER "questions the order" when transmitted correctly. So, you never think questions whether (the feeling of being aware does the person who accepts the suggestion itself), but simply the subconscious follows the order and obeys. And see, feel and perceive MULTI-sensuously that's true, that relaxation is taking place at that moment, and that is becoming more and more pleasant and enjoyable; then back again (I believe you ordered,

Then to continue with the induction and deepen the hypnotic state desired can continue saying something like "While you relax, I command you that your breathing fence becoming more and more calm, more and more serene ever". - "Every time you inhale, you breathe more and more quietly, and so with every breath you do, make your hypnotic trance is becoming more and more deep and pleasant for you." What do you think happens when that order is given? Well, as the body is already in the states of (WAVES ALFA / STATE = ALPHA Between 8 and 13 Hz, cycles per second or cps) means that are already relaxed automatically. And when the body relaxes, breathing itself is ALWAYS more calm, relaxed, deep and serene. But as the subconscious you are listening to what you say, he thinks he is through orders that what you're giving him what he does "carry out the order" and therefore the subconscious again your orders associated with the results; and poufs the hypnotic phenomenon begins to happen again, and the subconscious (CREE that "you're in charge" that "you're giving the orders" so that the second term that "Every time you breathe, you feel COMPLY each more and more relaxed and the more and more relaxed you feel, more and more hypnotized these, and the more and more hypnotized these, more and more come in, so deep, pleasant and enjoyable deep hypnotic state as the dream itself " . what makes you feel a deep sleep, and deep sleep that induces you to sleep NOW, so sleep) Do you understand the power of suggestion? Now do you understand the power to increase and increase Circle of Power or Strength Level to a higher level of authority at higher levels of hypnosis?

As we have learned so far. The hypnotic process; and hypnotic phenomena and hyper-suggestible subconscious ability to accept orders; It is as simple as the fact properly implement the orders in the circle or power level suitable Force. Ie carry out the orders correctly in the higher levels of authority; that is, at higher levels of HYPNOSIS at appropriate times and in appropriate and more favorable circumstances for the moment Are you really agree?

How we have seen so far, my dear readers, is simple to gradually increase our circle of power, or force level to a higher level of authority at higher levels of hypnosis. So, my invitation is that you get to work, begin to take action and make things happen. And I assure you that soon you will become the best hypnotist can become. *So, without further ado let's continue with the next chapter.*

CHAPTER VII BASIC TECHNIQUES APPLIED TO NLP HYPNOSIS NLP PSYCHOLINGUISTICS O

<u>CALIBRATION</u>: Calibration hypnosis is the ability to observe and recognize accurately and gradually the mental and emotional state of a person. And knowing when that same person is moving from one state to another. In other words, CALIBRATE in hypnosis is to detect various internal emotional states of mind. As well as facial and body micro expressions that people reflect in a given time. Calibration is produced from the recognition of the various external indicators with which people express their inner world through changes in their physiology and understanding, your mind map in a specific hypnotic state.

It is important to note at this point that all human behavior or conduct; is a neurological activity is determined by the feelings, experiences, INNER FEELINGS, THOUGHTS, maps and models of the world. And for that reason, it can be detected and (recognized). CALIBRATION being one of the most effective techniques of NLP applied to HYPNOSIS created and developed for this purpose.

Calibrated proper practice of hypnosis with NLP, can rightly guess, what is taking place inside the person (thoughts and emotions) and from there, to accompany him in the hypnotic process. This step represents a great opportunity to carry out a positive suggestion, or apply Hypnotic Persuaders patterns when the occasion requires it.

Persons wishing to properly use the calibration technique HYPNOSIS must first learn to "identify the various expressions of both language (verbal and nonverbal)". You must also learn to "recognize the different mental and emotional states and the discrepancy between thoughts and emotions, whether positive and negative". It is therefore vitally important to recognize the neurophysiological changes that occur within the individual states of trance, and reflected outwardly through small and subtle facial and body micro expressions both conscious and unconscious.

To develop our calibration capability to a higher level you have to learn to identify an integrated manner the various signals that present themselves subtly in the person such as: Body and micro-facial language, the rhythm of breathing "if deep or artificial, chest or abdominal "among others. To master the art of calibration hypnosis, you need to gradually develop expertise in the recognition of eye movements, pupil dilation and learn to detect the different tones of voice, heart rate, unconscious contractions skin and pores among other factors.

Therefore; to achieve this goal in hypnosis sessions, you must first promote a suitable environment of harmony, peace, tranquility and confidence, that allows us to observe the verbal and non-verbal language of the person. So that, by this means, we can detect and recognize the "levels or degrees of HYPNOSIS" by what's going on the subject in question. By looking both gestures, and postures; This can help us to discover gauge their internal behavior and the behavior associated with that mental and emotional state. And so, get in tune and more effectively rapport with him.

Guide to identify changes and emotional states in hypnotic states

THE BREATHING
- **Rhythm** *"Balanced or Uncontrolled " - "Slow or Suave"*
- **Shape** *"Abdominal or Pectoral"*
- **Volume** *"Sufficient or insufficient"*

EYE MOVEMENTS
- **vr:** *Upwards, towards the left.*
- **Vc:** *Upwards, towards the right.*
- **Ar:** *Laterally to the final point of the left eye.*
- **Ac:** *Laterally to the tip end of the right side of the eye.*
- **K:** *Downwards, towards the right.*
- **GAVE:** *Down in the right direction*

DILATATION
- *The "Pupil" - the "lower lip"*

MICRO-FACIAL EXPRESSIONS
- "Gestures or gestures" of doubt, fear, fear, anger, restlessness, tension, Relaxation, Excitement, Joy, security, happiness, peace, love and harmony.

BODY POSTURE
- *"Symmetry" - "Orientation" - "Tilt or cock"*

Head position, hand movements
- *"Movements of Affirmation" - "Movements of Denial"*
- *"Gestures with hands and fingers"*

MUSCULAR TONE
- *"Stressed or relaxed" - "gestural, expressive"*

TEMPERATURE, HUMIDITY AND SKIN COLOR
- **Perspiration** - *"Sweating - Dilation and Coloration of Pores"*

THE VOICE
- **Rhythm** *"Paused or fast"*
- **Doorbell** *"High or low"*
- **Tone** *"Smooth or Rough"*
- **Volume** *"High or low"*

sub modalities or PREDICATES VERBAL
- **Visual** *"Perceive your map through what you see and be seen"*
- **Auditory** *"Perceive your map through what you hear and you can hear"*
- **Kinesthetic** *"Perceive your map through which you can touch or feel"*

TRIMMING This strategy used in NLP hypnosis is to modify the framework by which a person perceives the facts, situations or contexts. Reframing then allows us to change this way the original meaning of a hypnotic experience that you have had or are experiencing; thus, allowing to create a new reality.

In other words, Reframing in hypnosis is the ability to learn to locate the possible framework of a person through memory, as well as imagination, intending to change the meaning of a certain frame of reference, either an event lived, experienced or created through hypnosis. And changing; size, smell, color, taste, shape, size, climate, among other sensory perceptions. Thus, enabling change, the emotional state, responses, behaviors and behavior of a particular individual, thus bringing the person to establish a new understanding, meaning and reality of the situation experienced in the hypnotic trance, generating an answering POSITIVE new and better hypnotic experience compared to the same event.

In another order of idea; TRIMMING applied technique allows re-induce hypnosis and redirect subjectively behaviors and unwanted behaviors of people, intending to capture the mood and emotional states of the subject. And then that same person driving a "altered state of consciousness HIGH" and improve their framework more assertive and positive in the state of hypnotic trance DESIRED way.

In this way, we more easily reach the subconscious of the person helping you change optimal, positively and effectively a certain way of thinking, feeling or acting, either of an event, behavior or situation, and allow him a new and better sense orientation to the situation.

I will share with you an example to illustrate the above idea. If you know some art; you'll have noticed that the artist, creating his masterpiece, not only play with the creativity of his painting, but when displaying it knows that the framework will have much influence on the rest of the picture.

That is to say; that if he wants to highlight a specific part of your work, you only have to frame your painting with a framework to subjectively people focus their gaze on a particular point. For example, if the picture frame is red, highlighted in painting whatever is reddish hue.

Similarly, it happens reframing technique. Used correctly in hypnosis, you can change the framework of the experience of a person, causing a change in radically different perspective of the same situation, creating a new mental map or a new reality at the same scene.

TRIMMING technique has many applications. FOR EXAMPLE: In the process of HYPNOTIC TRANCE you can apply the technique of CROP; raising awareness to the person, making him see that it has all the resources you need to change attitudes in a particular activity, in which present difficulties. It can be achieved, highlighting the positive part of that activity and the advantage you have, so that the individual deliberately changes the mode of the activity, and thus change the meaning of it had a more positive meaning. Allowing you to take action with a better attitude.

In condition Hypnotist or Mesmer; through my years of experiences in sections of therapeutic hypnosis or my shows hypnosis show with my coachees or participants, I learned that being in the best desired state possible (Inner Game) allows me to achieve much better results. And get this way, the person achieves enter a state of optimal, positive and provisions sessions or hypnotic trance show itself, making it possible technique TRIMMING do better in my participants.

As a hypnotherapist and hypnotist, I have learned that one must be a constant observer of the personality of the coachees or participants who are witnessing, intending to capture the moods they present, in terms of their activities in our sections of hypnosis or hypnosis street shows or shows. When I perceive that one of my coachees or participants do not have the motivation required at a specific point. I teach CROP, to achieve change the meaning of the assignment. And this allows, they perceive it in a more effective manner.

> *Sensory acuity will allow us to recognize the states of excellence of others; and will help us to strengthen them, allowing us to have the potential to leave anyone in a better state than when we started the initial contact.*

To improve results when applying any technique NLP hypnosis is necessary to take into account these fundamental principles:

OBJECTIVE: Knowing what I want to achieve and how I want to achieve, focusing on the goal and the purpose or objective to be achieved.

sensory acuity: Be alert and keep your senses alert; so that we realize what is happening inside and outside our coachees. And so, determine the results being obtained. Detecting properly, if what I do about me or me away from my goal.

FLEXIBILITY: Ability to be changing the way they act, or apply the techniques of hypnosis, until the required results are obtained. Timely changing what prevents us from achieving what we really want to achieve.

<u>ANCHORAGE</u>: The ANCHOR in hypnosis is the process by which an external stimulus is associated with a behavior or response that is to be generated. FOR EXAMPLE: Playing (kinesthetic contact) any specific body part (arm / hand) the subject "patient or participant" whenever we want to encourage him to feel (relaxed); make a gesture (movement) specific to approve or disapprove a certain action; declare or decree a specific keyword (SLEEPS) order to generate a given state (SLEEP), display some event (imagine a situation), hear a melody or a voice specified (hearing a particular sound) or a combination of hypnotic elements both. By applying the technique correctly, both bind and then the brain does all the work.

You can also set an external stimulus (ANCHOR) and link it intentionally with a hypnotic experience, in order to attract her and revive her at the time you want. This is properly the process ANCHOR in its practical illustration. It is similar to what in some branches of Behavioral Psychology is known as Conditioned Reflex or conditioning of reflexes by a sensory stimulus.

This system Conditioned Reflex was studied by Russian researcher Ivan Pávlov. *Through which, demonstrated that this procedure ANCHOR STIMULUS - RESPONSE mobilizes valid experiences through conscious or subconscious suggestions that later could be used successfully in required previously prepared and established for this purpose situations.* **(In our case apply ANCHOR** "Stimulus - response" to a hypnotic PHENOMENON).

In the late nineteenth century, the Russian physiologist Ivan Pávlov name (1849-1936), Nobel Prize (1904), first demonstrated what we now know as the law of CONDITIONAL REFLEX, which by an error in the translation of his work English language was called "Conditioned Reflex" and popularized in different fields of behavioral psychology as "conditioning of reflexes" classical conditioning or learning partnerships. And today those same procedures used in the practice of hypnosis.

Classical conditioning applied to hypnosis, is a type of learning and behavior that is to connect a natural stimulus to its natural response, and then anchored with a second stimulus caused to generate a hypnotic response that does not naturally occur. Otherwise, classical conditioning applied to hypnosis is the simplest mechanism by which generate hypnotics phenomena related to a Stimuli - Responses. This conditioning of reflexes allows humans to induce certain stimuli and physiological well-being, automatic, involuntary emotional or psychological responses that can then be anchored to a previously established situation.

The best-known classic example of all is that of the famous Pavlov's dogs. *It was simply to ring a bell before feeding dogs. ENCOURAGEMENT repeatedly produced, food - bell, bell - food ... And by repeating the same stimulus again and again to create a response.* What made then was to remove one of the stimuli (the food), and noted that after the expiry of a period of time when only the bell rang, the animal body react as if there was food. That is, produced "secreted" a lot of saliva and somehow responded positively to the campaign, but this time he was presenting food. Ivan Pávlov through this experiment of classical conditioning found to be induced in animals and humans to react involuntarily to a stimulus - response that previously had no effect, and now through learning partnerships encouragement to achieve eventually produce or generate a conditioned response automatically.

In the practice of hypnosis or hypnotism PSYCHOLINGUISTICS PNL; the usefulness of this procedure known as conditioning reflexes or (Theory Pávlov) is used for behavior modification through the technique called "ANCHOR" consisting produce a particular sensory stimulus to instantly awaken a particular response which makes possible "{(MOBILIZE)}" or "{(INDUCE)}" valid and full of resource states hypnotic experiences that allow the subject (patient or participant) addressing a specific situation with greater assurance of success. Hypnotherapeutic context understood a "success" as the ability to achieve previously established hypnotic phenomena.

So, I learned above, we can say that an anchor applied to hypnosis is an association or (Linking Intentional) of something that is created between certain thoughts, ideas, feelings, feelings and altered states of consciousness (Answers) and "{(SIGNAL)} "certain sensory (stimulus) either character Auditory, visual or kinesthetic. For that reason; In hypnosis using the NLP technique called ANCHOR we can learn to associate and connect PHENOMENA HYPNOTICS by (sensory signals) through the senses. Which can be either be words, gestures, sounds, touches, gestures, signs, souvenirs, visualizations, images, melodies, rhythms, etc.

In another order of ideas; Anchoring is a simple, but effective hypnotic sensory process that enables you to transform negative emotions into positive sensations through the appropriate use of the technique of conditioned reflex. When you create a program ANCHOR Responses to respond positively to a given stimulus when needed.

ANCHOR technique applied to hypnosis, usually introduced in connection with an issue known as "Peak Moment", ie any individual life situation that is particularly intense emotionally for him. How, for example, could be: Feeling happy, cheerful, happy, feeling absolute pleasure, be completely relaxed or focused on something or someone. I want to imply; It is that any particular sensory impression is capable of serving as anchor or "BOOST" to {(remember)}, {(attract)}, {(mobilize)} or {(induce)} an experience "ANSWER". As may be the case of a certain action, voice, feeling, induction, or a splash in particular, among others. These anchors are stimuli associated with such emotional or mental states.

5 Steps to Creating an Effective Hypnotic ANCHOR

1) <u>Identify the hypnotic state we want to generate</u>: That can be peace, relaxation, etc. This step is crucial because you need to clearly define the feeling you want to feel (relaxation), and encouragement would induce (peace). You must always do it in the present tense and positive. For example: "You are completely relaxed." Always keep in mind that you must first preselect the feeling (relaxation) stimulus you want ANCHOR and then generate the response (peace). And I do always decisive and positive way.

2) <u>It causes particular sensation (relaxation) stimulus and generates the response you want to induce (inner peace)</u>: To achieve produce is very important ANCHOR relive his past, and you stimulate memories in your mind or resources that have experienced the desired hypnotic state needs. (Inner peace and relaxation).

3) <u>DESIRED creates the hypnotic state</u>: Using either visualization, imagination, memories or suggestion. To do this, you must stimulate in the subject feeling (relaxation) you have chosen ANCHOR as if happening in the here and now. Concentrating on the feeling you want to induce (inner peace) through sensory stimuli (visual, auditory, kinesthetic). Ie activate all sensations and multisensory stimuli response you want to provoke.

4) <u>Anchoring set</u>: Look at the desired emotional state of the subject when you reach the "Peak Moment" active anchor. Repeat this process 5 times, and each "Moment Summit" in which the desired state of emotions the subject is at its peak, creates the anchor. That can be through a kinesthetic signal you perform with the touch of your hands, while at the same time you utter a keyword that induce the desired auditory stimulus (relax deeply), and finally activates its visual channel by means of an image or a memory that represents the visual state to be desired induce (peace). All these three elements must be interconnected ANCHORS each other. Most important of this exercise is that you stimulate the mind and body experience the hypnotic subject you want induce.

5) <u>Repeat point 4 five 5 times to consolidate the ANCHOR created</u> This repetition is essential and important. For this reason, you should do it repeatedly several times throughout the session or the hypnotic show. And at least provoke between 7-21 times consecutive, until you have strengthened the ANCHOR positively to it.

RAPPORT The term comes from the French RAPPORT "rapporter" which means to accomplish something. The Rapport in Hypnosis allows us acompass and create an illusion of mirroring in order to establish an empathy with people with whom we are working, thus facilitating the hypnotic process between the two sides. The RAPPORT applied correctly in HYPNOSIS with LEADING technique allows us to guide the proper context to establish optimal highly effective communication at the time that a connection or interaction when stimulated or creating hypnotic phenomena is established.

For HYPNOSIS, Rapport or "pacing" is the ability to adapt or accommodate a situation, context or circumstance to establish rapport, harmony, affinity and agreement on both the verbal language, such as non-verbal regarding the interpersonal relationship between the subject (patient or participant) and Hypnotist, Mesmer, hypnologist or Hypnotherapist. In order to create an emotional connection with the mental state of the other person. If their Rapport, communication between the two parties has more fluid, thus producing a greater harmony and pacing both between their bodies and minds, and in their words, actions, gestures, thoughts and physiologies.

In another idea, we could define RAPPORT "As the process through which you can establish rapport and contact with others in a conscious and unconscious level at the same time." We could also say that Rapport is the science that allows us to feel comfortable with each other, and at the same time make others feel comfortable can be with us.

Rapport is a very interesting technique in hypnosis. This particular technique gives us the ability to create an enabling environment for more effective communication with people with whom we work context; whether they are in our sessions of therapeutic hypnosis, or hypnosis shows our shows. Anyway; to reinforce the idea, we could define rapport as the ability and skill that has the human being to stand in the place of the other person and understand. At the same time to allow the other person feels the same empathy and affinity towards us. Thus, allowing that this more open to a more pleasant, sincere, open and enjoyable for both effective communication, resulting in a win - win communication and our daily interactions.

LEADING and calibrate as tools to facilitate rapport in hypnosis How do we know if we are in harmony in a session or hypnotic show? How do we know that we are in tune with the other person? LEADING: It means "guide" and calibrate a person means knowing a person through verbal and non-verbal language its internal state. Namely, your mood or mental state and keep it in mind throughout the process of the session or the hypnotic show. The Leading then it allows us to guide the hypnotic interaction while the Equipment Calibration allows us to confirm if we are correctly realizing the Rapport.

<u>How to perform properly Rapport technique to generate a desired HYPNOTIC STATE OF TRANCE?</u>

The method is very simple, we just get our (patient or participant) feel comfortable and safe and confident on our side; ie familiar with the process and guided by us. And how do we do that? The simplest way to get subject (patient or participant) with whom we are interacting, see before him a hypnotist, Hypnotist, hypnotist or hypnotherapist who find it professional, skilled and competent with hypnotic process we are leading. And how is this possible, give effect to this result to the optimal levels? Through the technique of mirroring. Which is a very subtle way to copy and duplicate similarly all the gestures, mannerisms, attitudes, emotions, rhythm, tone of voice and hypnotic phenomena that we generate in our party (patient or participant).

The RAPPORT in hypnosis is a technique of sync, that aim to create a deeper connection with hypnotic trance state of the subject (patient or participant). Imagine the following situation, for example: Imagine seeing a couple of artists performing a tango dance in complete harmony and synchronization at each step, the rhythm and beat of the music. It is as if the two dancers merged such that each was in step with the other guide or synergistically, holistic, complementary and integral manner simultaneously.

Rapport alone; often it occurs spontaneously between couples, friends and acquaintances. Rapport also generated in different contexts, situations or circumstances, either in our relationships or our relationship (patient / doctor) or (participant and hypnotist). For this reason, we could say with certainty that the Rapport in hypnosis serves to create good impressions in our therapeutic clinical hypnosis sessions or at our shows of street hypnosis or show. So, using the Rapport technique in our procedures HYPNOTICS intelligently and properly so, we allow more positively influence our relationships with our (patients or participants).

> But WARNING! The rapport in hypnosis requires delicacy, intuition, subtlety and above all respect. It is imperative to establish rapport correctly, be subtle and use mostly common sense to dock with and modestly acompass movements of the subject (patients or participants) similarly. *But without trying to imitate mockingly our interlocutor, much less parody exactly the person with whom we are working. Since this type of unconscious actions could backfire and create an adverse reaction to that hope.*

In short, as an allegorical example we can add that:

Scientifically proven our central nervous system, is like a network or fiber optic cabling. Once we get to understand how the network or OPTICAL SYSTEM WIRING one functions; We understand better how to access your neural network or SENSORY SYSTEM WIRING SUBCONSCIOUS; and send the information (instructions, orders, suggestions, guidance or inductions) we want to successfully reach your subconscious through the representational system that the subject (patients or participants) better master. And thus, achieve a better connection in the hypnotic process we are heading.

For that we must learn to be calibrated correctly and recognize the different sub-modalities (visual, auditory and kinesthetic) and eyepieces ACCESS to thus have greater input to its neural network or system of sensory optical cabling and thus generate better RAPPORT in our interactions.

One of the fastest and most effective rapport in hypnosis techniques is to look at the "{ACCESS EYEPIECES}" or eye movements and establish our dialogue through the "{sub modality}" or representational systems that are using the subject (patients or participants) at that time.

FOR EXAMPLE: If you look up when talking means it is a visual person and we could talk using visual images, if you look with your eyes horizontally, sideways means that it is a hearing person and talk using words that represent sounds, and if, on the contrary, he looks with your eyes looking down means that surely is a kinesthetic or sensory person and in those cases, he would speak using words that represent emotions and feelings.

<u>Eye accessing cues used in HYPNOSIS</u>

EYE ACCESS keys: the movements (lateral, vertical and horizontal) that they are made through our eyes; while we produce or generate "{sensations, emotions, thoughts or memories}" naturally activating systems or REPRESENTATION SENSORY Sub modalities "visual, auditory and kinesthetic." (Visual what we see, what we hear auditory, kinesthetic or sensory what we touch, feel, smell and taste ") process we do all the people most of the time, unconsciously or involuntarily.

It is vital to note at this point; the eye movement, are to be considered from the point of view of the observer (Hypnotist, Mesmer, hypnologist or Hypnotherapist). Namely, as if they were looking straight ahead, face to face the subject (patients or participants). And these eye accesses are applicable to the vast majority of individuals. While we must invest in the few exceptional cases that exist in some left-handed people, even some skillful in which some schemes may be reversed into its opposite, but the latter are only exceptions.

Observation of eye movements offers one of the fastest and effective means we know hypnosis to determine at all times; how the person (patients or participants) builds its internal experience or altered state of consciousness. Correctly applied the technique in hypnosis allows us to accurately recognize the particular channel or representational sub modality you are using the subject (patients or participants) to produce hypnotic phenomena being experienced at that particular time.

By using this information properly in our favor, we empower better identify the construction of mental and psychological processes that are going on the subject (patients or participants) through observing the different positions or movements of the eyes that person in question is causing unconsciously in different degrees or levels of hypnotic phenomena.

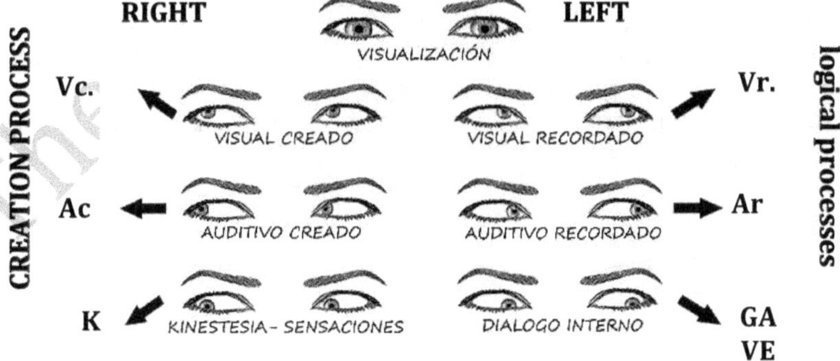

How EYE ACCESS keys work in hypnosis? The eye accessing cues are certain types of unconscious Micro expressions associated with our behavior, that activate our neurology running certain bodily functions, in this case EYE MOVEMENTS our eyes in different directions representing "SYSTEMS sensory representation or Sub modalities" either " visual, Auditory, Kinesthetic ".

ALLEGORICAL EXAMPLE function as a shift lever in an automobile gearbox synchronously; such as a (Ferrari for you to imagine a model carriage) to associate with this allegory. Depending on where you put the gear lever (positions of gaze of your eyes) have access to the different speeds (Sub modalities the representational system) either are these "visual, auditory or kinesthetic sensory"

The information offered by this tool correctly applied in hypnosis lets us know the representation of the world map being used by the subject (patients or participants) in a given hypnotic state. Since the eye movement allows us to focus on the predominant channel or representational system being used by the person concerned; and use this information to our advantage, to generate orders, instructions, inductions and suggestions coupled to the unconscious process that the person is experiencing at that moment.

Here I share a pattern of orientation, which can be used in conjunction with the image of the previous page to help guide you.

Guidelines to correctly identify the keys to access the HYPNOSIS EYE

Vr: Visual Remembered: We put eyes looking up, towards the Left.
Vc: Visual Created or Imagined: We put eyes looking up toward the right.
Ar: Auditory Recalled: We look laterally toward the tip end side of the Left Eye.
Ac: Auditive Created or Remembered: We looked laterally toward the tip end of the right side of the eye.
K: Kinesthetic - Sensory: We place downgaze in clockwise direction.
GAVE: Internal dialogue: We place downgaze, towards the Left.

sub modalities: Sub modalities of representative systems applied to hypnosis, are the different variables that belong to the same access perception we use "Outwardly to perceive the world - e- internally to represent them in the form of experience" and defining the difference in how we process, store and encode different hypnotic phenomena and processes we are experiencing through the "different sensory channels" (VAK- "O and G"). Visual what we see, what we hear auditory, kinesthetic or sensory what we touch and feel, "Olfactory and Gustatory what we smell or taste what we taste."

It is impossible to think of a particular situation of our life or recall a life experience without this having a structure in sub modalities, ie without coming into play processes sensory perceptions such as (sight, hearing, touch, taste and smell).

Let me give you an allegorical example to reinforce the previous idea.

GO FIGURE a film director who to give greater impact to your movies when shooting changes, the lighting and angle of your camera a crucial scene to another to cause us a stimulus. Or do we listen to certain music, noise or background sound depending on the feelings and emotions that wants to awaken in us, all in conjunction with the performances of the actors and actresses in staging we communicate a message through their bodily expressions and verbal and non-verbal communication; that give us either, fear, horror, suspense, drama, pain, sadness, joy, happiness, love, passion, excitement, sensuality, or desire. Anyway, a lot of situations that produce an answer in our body. And this happens within us, which plays a critical role in our subconscious mind through sensory representations (visual, auditory or kinesthetic) is what we call sub modalities hypnosis.

As we learned in the previous example sub modalities in hypnosis are always present in the processed of thoughts and emotions that unconsciously activated by sensory representations when receiving an order either (see, hear, feel, smell and taste) any situation. Place in the subject (patients or participants) a response in the body (hypnotic phenomenon) we want to induce.

It is important to note at this point that: The human being uses filters to create the map of the territory of their reality, in order to understand the world and delimit. So far, I have stated 5 that are the primary filters (visual, auditory, kinesthetic or sensory, smell and taste), but within each of these broad categories in turn, there are more subtle ranges in the human mind. What we call sub modalities hypnosis of thought.

For practical purposes Hypnosis works with the 3 main Sub modalities namely Visual, Auditory, Kinesthetic or sensory impairment. Although there are people who develop the other two sub modalities. Olfactory and gustatory with much greater intensity than normal. But these two (2) last Sub modalities fall into the category kinesthetic or sensory impairment.

From now on, we will refer only to these 3 primary Sub modalities (visual, auditory and kinesthetic sensory). Here I will present a list of Sub Modalities Visual, auditory, and kinesthetic, and a general list of questions to detect the different sub modalities in each individual, so champions and champions; it gets from good to better, so let's continue ...

<u>CHARACTERISTICS OF SENSORY REPRESENTATION SYSTEMS "visual, auditory, kinesthetic" applied to the HYPNOSIS</u>

<u>THE VISUALS</u>: Are all those people and subjects (patients or participants) that show sessions or hypnosis prefer visual stimuli. And more clearly, they identified with "what COME AND DISTINGUISHED THROUGH THE SENSE OF SIGHT". Are people and subjects (patients or participants) who like to watch as they speak, detailing what happens around them, they like to be looked into her eyes as they give orders, suggestions and inductions. That is, they feel more comfortable when they see that they are paying due attention they deserve; when being redirected or induce to produce a specific HYPNOTIC phenomenon.

<u>hearing</u>: Are all those people and subjects (patients or participants) than in the hypnosis sessions or show favor Audible Stimuli. Since identify more with words, sounds and spoken descriptions. That is, they feel more identified with "what they hear and be heard melodiously". Upon receipt of orders, suggestions and inductions are identified regularly hear more when hearing instructions tone, rhythm and volume of voice appropriate to allow them to recreate the hypnotic phenomena are suggesting them.

<u>kinesthetic</u>: Are all those people and subjects (patients or participants) than in the sessions or hypnosis show preferred sensory stimuli. Since they identify more with the Contact Body and somehow interested in your feelings and nearby approaches made by the (Hypnotist, Hypnotist, hypnotist or hypnotherapist). You can notice them much more comfortable with "what they feel and perceive THROUGH EMOTIONS multisensory" in its communication often are what have slower movements, feel comfortable expressing their feelings openly, like the touch and are very affectionate when they perceive that they correspond properly during sessions or hypnosis show.

CHAPTER VIII: TESTS SUGGESTIBILITY, COVERT TESTING, INDUCTIONS, CONVENCERS AND UNITED DOWNRIGGERS HYPNOTICS

Well champions and champions have reached the eighth and final chapter of this book. Hereinafter; This section of the book, I will share some of the suggestibility tests, undercover tests, inductions, convencers and downriggers most known and effective when creating and producing high-hypnotic phenomena hypnotic states.

> **IMPORTANT NOTE**: Remember that this first book, was aimed at you teach to master and understand the first principles so you could begin to "know, practice, exercise and perform HYPNOSIS" ... If you want to delve deeper into these techniques and methodology in a profound way, you can do through the second and third part of this series, which I divided in 3 volumes ... and this work; is only the first of 3 books ... I wrote to you, in order to end that by reading the trilogy COMPLETES you really can become the hypnotist you want and you can become ...

So, without further ado let's begin. To begin this initial lesson; first we see a few things that are vital to know before entering the best of this last chapter, which is the understanding of the basic and advanced techniques of hypnosis before, during and after the session or show.

Part One: hypnosis session as the Point of View of the beholder

To start, I will begin by describing how the development of a hypnosis session, from the point of view of the subject (viewer) patient or participant:

When starting the hypnosis session, most likely the subject (viewer) patient or participant at first may be that this a little distracted or focused on the expectations you have about what will or may happen. This process can begin mostly sitting, lying or standing, as applicable.

Chances are that if you have some degree of experience in a previous hypnosis session will probably be relaxed and thinking normally what you should do shortly. If the contrary is your first time, you might at first feel some degree of anxiety, curiosity and have some questions regarding what you believe or think is or is not hypnosis. All these reactions or behaviors are normal, and we must keep them in mind at all times, to carry the hypnosis session to the next level.

*In the beginning of the hypnosis session the subject (viewer) patient or participant, it is in the NORMAL STATE OF ALERT or wakeful state (Z0). This conscious state is characterized by a high frequency or brain waves in neuronal activity BETA ranging from 14 to 28**Hz (Cycles per second or cps)***

Once you have logged in hypnosis, the subject (viewer) patient or participant, will be in the process of transition from the normal waking state (Z0) The State HIPNOIDAL or Incantation (Z0 and Z1). Semi-conscious state, characterized by decreasing the frequency levels or brain waves in neuronal activity ALPHA / ALPHA ranging from 8 to 13**Hz (Cycles per second or cps)**

Once the subject (viewer) patient or participant has finished hearing the pre-hypnotic talk has responded therapeutic script, performs first tests Suggestibility, has executed some basic suggestions, you have met some orders of a CIRCLE Power or Force FP1 level and complete some orders level or higher FP2 Authority. Then the subject (viewer) patient or participant, we'll be ready to move to the next level.

To raise the subject (viewer) patient or participant to the next level and achieve our goal can do so using one of the methods most popular and effective induction, for example: Dave Elman induction model. Once achieved our purpose, the subject (viewer) patient or participant enters the next state of mild hypnotic trance Superficial Z1. This semi-conscious state, is characterized by a greater decrease in the frequency levels or brain waves in neuronal activity ZETA / THETA ranging from 6 to 7**Hz (Cycles per second or cps).**

In this state Z1 the subject (viewer) patient or participant knows that he is still semi-conscious. So sometimes doubt is in a state of hypnosis, and listening to the hypnotist and perceives everything that happens in their surroundings and environment around him. As this state is very unstable, and the individual always tends to return to normal waking state. For this reason, it is advisable that during this period, the hypnotist, Hypnotist, hypnotist or hypnotherapist must take into account the switch and deepen with audible, tactile and visual techniques to bring the person to the next level of hypnotic trance MEDIUM or cataleptic Z1 and Z2. This state of semi-major unconsciousness **Hz (Cycles per second or cps)** outwardly perceptible.

Now from here, it happens a very interesting fact. By increasing the circle of power, or Strength Level (FP3 and FP4), and has completed some commands authority level or higher FP5 and above. Then the subject (viewer) patient or participant, we'll be ready to move to the next higher grade advanced level.

Upon entering the subject (viewer) patient or participant in this state of deep hypnotic trance state known as somnambulistic THRESHOLD HYPNOTIC TRANCE Z2. This state is the most hypnotic trance reached, and is characterized by a greater degree in reducing the frequency levels or brain waves in neuronal activity DELTA ranging from 0.5 to 3 Hz or (cycles per second or fps), which is externally perceptible clarity compared to the previous ones.

It is important to note at this point that (By conducting covert tests, convencers and techniques deepening hypnotic states) the subject (viewer) patient or participant, began to have moments of disorientation, resulting in a temporary erase from your events perceived by your conscious mind. What will make the subject (viewer) patient or participant forget temporarily or sporadically covert tests, convencers and deepening techniques that induce hypnotic states and brought into that state of deep hypnotic trance.

Saying that he erases or forget temporarily or sporadically certain events, I mean that when I wake up the subject and return to your state of alertness (alertness or wakefulness), if we asked you to tell us everything you remember since the beginning of the hypnosis session, will remember only so far before, what brought him into the state of deep hypnotic trance.

__FOR EXAMPLE__: Suppose we started giving suggestions and direct inductions your left arm will be very, very light, and when it is very light, it starts to levitate, float, rise up and unconsciously through the power of his mind. Then we accompanied him a disguised test a downrigger to give you a direct order to the left arm to bend and approaches her face slowly until the touch. Then we continue with the suggestions of a circle or power level Force (FP3 and FP4). And when we have deepened the experience and the subject (viewer) patient or participant has completed the orders of a higher level of authority or higher level FP5 and ordered to fall asleep. So, at this time,

Then when you wake up and return to their state of alertness (alertness or wakefulness) and ask you to tell us what you remember. This will only remember your hand up. (Will forget and was erased temporarily or sporadically specific action that brought him into the state of deep hypnotic trance. That is, you forget that your left hand touches his face and fell asleep) Yes, the person knows that there is something more, but you cannot remember, when asked "what do you remember the word 'face'?" that he forgot he will come to mind and remember it perfectly ...

> **IMPORTANT**: While the subject (viewer) patient or participant is in the THRESHOLD HYPNOTIC STATE OF TRANCE somnambulistic Z2 (deep), everything that happens not remember, unless we indicate you are to remember it.

May on rare occasions, and rarely that during the hypnosis session, the subject (viewer) patient or participant if new to hypnotic procedures, it is inexperienced or is very, very tired, exhausted, upset and He stressed for some reason; which of course it can happen. These above reasons, you can do enter the state Z3 (State Very Deep Reverie); If this phenomenon happens, you will notice very easily, seeing that the subject does not respond to our suggestions and see it even really sleep (literal or physiologically) talking. In this state Z3 (Condition Very Deep Reverie), the subject even once awakes, he cannot remember anything that has happened at this stage. (Although it reminds us) and the reason is simple and easy "It was because he fell asleep,

This is logical, and it is very clear. It's like trying to remember a sleepwalker (who speaks and walks while asleep) remember what he did or said while asleep. Is it impossible right? Well the same is true in this state Z3 (State Very Deep Reverie).

Part Two: HYPNOSIS SESSION according Viewpoint Mesmer

Now to continue, I will describe a hypnosis session from the point of view of the specialist (hypnotist) hypnotist or hypnotherapist:

We can divide it into 5 stages:
1. **Induce**;
2. **Deepen**;
3. **Hypnotic Trance phenomena or**;
4. **Suggestion** Posthypnotic or intervention;
5. **Procedure Awakening**;

1. Induce: It means placing the subject in the state Z1.
2. Deepen: Corresponds to make you pass the state Z2.
*3. Hypnotic Trance phenomena or: This is the level where the set target is reached (heal an ailment, learn or teach a skill, overcome a habit or develop a more empowered, to create anesthesia, analgesia, catalepsy, etc.) thanks to have succeeded in increasing the **CIRCLE OF POWER** or Level Strength (FP3 and FP4) to a higher level of authority or higher FP5 and Higher*
4. Posthypnotic suggestion of Intervention: The essential element of hypnosis. It is when the subject (viewer) patient or participant It is in the transition between states Z1 to Z2, and we can give posthypnotic orders that extend and run once you've awakened. And orders remain in force once the session is complete, even on days or later dates.

> *This is very interesting, I'll share an example: "From now on, whenever you touch the forehead (creating a kinesthetic anchor - touch with your hands) and tell you to sleep (create an auditory anchor - with the word SLEEPS) you enter a state of deep hypnotic trance even more, which you are now (create a sensory anchor - feel completely relaxed). Now, to prove that you understood, accepted and assimilated everything I've told you, I'm going to count to three (3) and wake up. And you will see that you will find you well and you will feel full of energy and vitality; but whenever you touch the forehead and tell you to sleep, close your eyes and go into a state of hypnosis further and deeper. Story: 1're regaining your energy and vitality; 2 you are very good and you feel sensational, and you're waking up more and more; 3 you can wake up active and ready to continue, awake now. "...*
>
> *ONCE CREATED THE ORDER; and the subject (viewer) patient or participant wakes up, test the suggestion posthypnotic will pass the slight hand and gently across the face (activating the kinesthetic anchor) and tell SLEEPS (activating auditory and sensory anchor) and if the person understood, accept and assimilate the entire order was to be implemented before, re-enter the state of deep hypnotic trance agreed. AND READY have achieved the goal you understand the idea? Do you understand the potential of posthypnotic suggestion? ...*

<u>5.</u> *Procedure Awakening*. The process of awakening, is the most important at the end of our hypnotic session, as it is the action that allows us to cancel all that has been practiced or enacted in the hypnosis session. But keeping only the posthypnotic suggestion if any. For this reason, because of its importance, this must be done or done slowly, and never awaken the subject(Viewer) patient or participant and a fast or abruptly. Most ideally, as follows: "When I count to three (3) awaken the state in which you are now, and you wake up alert, ready, attentive and energy and welfare 100% of your optimum performance, you're READY "Story: 1're regaining your energy and vitality! 2 you are very good and you feel sensational, and you're waking up and activating your 5 senses growing; 3 you can wake up and active and ready to continue, awake now. "...

<u>NOTE</u>: *As we begin the process of awakening, it is advisable while we counting (1, 2, 3 ...) gradually increase the tone and volume of our voice and engage our pace and rhythm of what we are saying in consistency feeling, emotion and experience that we are inducing the person. Thus, the subject (viewer) Vera patient or participant in our words, actions and expressions experiences we want to convey.*

SYNTHESIS "Before, During and After a hypnosis session"

1.   **BEFORE THE HYPNOSIS** Make a previous interview, have a pre-hypnotic talk, write the medical report, read and complete the therapeutic script with the patient or participant, fill the contract or posthypnotic agreement to keep in mind the goals they want to achieve with the session, deepen the reason for the consultation or session, ask questions on the subject to locate possible psychological and physiological if any problems, detect fears, traumas, phobias, expectations, desires and interests, etc. Do you understand what I'm saying? By doing all this, you can not only prevent any problems with time, but above all you can come on and cover any expectation, positioning yourself as an expert in the field and strengthen your image as Hypnotist, Hypnotist, hypnotist or hypnotherapist. It is clear, that having a profile of the staff concerned who are going to work, you'll have more advantages, if not you would fulfill with all these initial procedures do I give me to understand? You agree that, by having more information, more likely to have success in carrying out your therapeutic clinical hypnosis sessions and more likely to have success to make your shows of street hypnosis or show. Are you clear on this truth? Knowing this, you'll avoid someone who has a phobia to water the method of the boat. XD - very careful with that. more likely to have success in carrying out your therapeutic clinical hypnosis sessions and more likely to have success to make your shows of street hypnosis or show. Are you clear on this truth? Knowing this, you'll avoid someone who has a phobia to water the method of the boat. XD - very careful with that. more likely to have success in carrying out your therapeutic clinical hypnosis sessions and more likely to have success to make your shows of street hypnosis or show. Are you clear on this truth? Knowing this, you'll avoid someone who has a phobia to water the method of the boat. XD - very careful with that.

2. **During hypnosis**: Induce, deepen, creating hypnotic phenomena, perform post-hypnotic suggestion, successfully complete the procedures of awakening, Increase Circle of Power or Strength Level one (FP1, FP2 and FP3) to a higher level of authority or higher FP5 and higher , testing suggestibility, covert tests, inductions, convencers and downriggers of hypnotic states, choose the state of hypnotic trance we want to achieve according to our goals (STATE HIPNOIDAL or Incantation Z0 and Z1, TRANCE HYPNOTIC MILD or Superficial Z1, TRANCE HYPNOTIC MEDIUM or cataleptic Z1 and Z2 or Z2 somnambulistic THRESHOLD HYPNOTIC TRANCE as appropriate.

3. **After hypnosis**: Have a short conversation with the subject (viewer) patient or participant, which prompted the person that has chronologically everything you remember that happened, as this allows us to detect the Z2 states, through amnesia retroactive and spontaneous posthypnotic. (This is called the temporary oblivion said before, that when entering Z2, forgot or technique that made him into a deep state (Z2) is deleted), ending a brief interview and check the contract or posthypnotic agreement verify that the objectives were met, schedule the next appointment, plan the next session of clinical or therapeutic hypnosis, planning the

next show of street hypnosis or hypnosis show , recommend, offer and sell some of your teaching materials and support (Audios, Videos, Books,

Now to know covert tests, tests of suggestibility, the convincing and profundizando states ...

These techniques in its many variants, in one way or another belong to one of the various categories Families hypnosis as "{[Eric Barone and Jacques Mandorla in his ABC of Hypnosis (Develop Your Mental Potential) Editions Tikal describe 8]} ". We will study only 4 of them that are considered the most practical, effective and powerful. These include: (sensory, physiological, Psicoimaginaria and Psicoconflictiva).

These techniques in any different families; they are made and combining subtly throughout the course of our hypnosis sessions or show our shows, through certain covert methodologies that we use as hypnotists wisely, to make our process easier in practice of hypnosis.

Thus, by these family's hypnosis "Sensory, Physiological, Psicoimaginaria and Psicoconflictiva" prepare the person, pre-Suggestion was the subject in his belief that the therapy session or entertainment show will be held successfully. That is, that through these techniques or covert testing, suggestibility, convencers and deepening states do "(believe, feel and experience)" the person concerned is living what is real. In other words, these techniques of suggestion and induction, serve to check the status of hyper-suggestibility of the subject, and to use them to our advantage, to produce the (desired state of trance) and thus generate hypnotic phenomena.

> **Let us sum** *One of the essential things you need to get here (during the tests, convencers and downriggers of states) is enabled on the person your HIPER-suggestibility, (ability to receive orders, suggestions and inductions) that will finally allow the subject believe, feel and experience that hypnosis is real, and it is possible to be hypnotized ...*

What follows below; are a number of techniques and methods to produce and generate both physical reactions (ideomotor, ideosensoriales or ideoemocionales), Physiologic (or natural response organic function body) and psychological (sugestionabilidad or inductive response created by our mind and thoughts). We will use as mental exercises induction, to achieve our goal (Hypnotize). These 4 families of hypnosis (sensory, physiological, Psicoimaginaria and Psicoconflictiva) are the first rung of the Hypnotic ladder and must be learned and understood well enough to perform the various covert tests, suggestibility, convencers and deepening of states that will study continuation.

COVERT TESTS, SUGGESTIBILITY, CONVENCERS AND UNITED DEEPENING HYPNOTICS.

The first technique we will know, is the magnetic FINGERS FAMILY SENSORIAL. As I discussed earlier, this type of tool subtly allows us to evaluate the degree of hyper-suggestibility of the person ... This technique of magnetic fingers or Paid has two components a physiological, and other sensory component ...

The technique of magnetic FINGERS, this substantiated (2) methodologies.
"1 Physiological" organ function or body's natural response
"2nd Sensorial" Inductive Response Suggestibility or Psychological
   ✓ ***Create a situation*** *of which we know the psychological consequences.*
   ✓ *It allows us to synchronize through suggestion.*
   ✓ *It allows us to divert suggestion towards a certain goal.*

SENSORY Family

This family includes all sensory techniques using procedures such as (technique of eye fixation mainly proposed *James Braid*).

*This technique Sensory FAMILY, they should take into account the visual perceptions "fixating"(Hypnotics discs, pendulums or strobe lamps, **color fringing**). Auditory perceptions "tone" (rhythm, style and rhythm); all tactile perceptions "Physical Contact Kinesthetic" also be used (**body posture**, Look, mannerisms, gestures, facial micro-expressions, verbal and nonverbal) among others. Because all these procedures, our eyes look different techniques actually obey the following strategy **SENSORY FAMILY**:*

*(**Let's see how these methods synergistically, holistic and comprehensive work**) ...* **Take an example of this SENSORIAL STRATEGY:**

CREATE A SITUATION IN WHICH THE CONSEQUENCES KNOWN PSYCHOLOGICAL. When we put clasped hands with index fingers raised in a "V", we know that certain attraction between them will appear. Sensory and physiological function that comes into play in magnetic FINGERS is simple, as the tendons of the fingers are tight, causes the tendons in the index fingers move and come together, automatically allying with each other ... and that the effect hypnotic wish Already understand the idea?

> **TRICK** As you see, we try to create a situation in which we know the consequences, and then attribute these consequences to which you want to sleep. (Actually, there is no relationship, but we must make him believe that if any)
>
> **FOR EXAMPLE**: In the test of the magnetic FINGERS, we know that when someone is holding hands, adjusted and index fingers raised in a "V" about 2 to 3 centimeters ... Sooner or later it will attract each other. If we say that first will win his fingers and attract; when you say you will start to stick, they are stick together! Do you see how easy it is? ...

SYNCHRONIZE THROUGH THE SUGGESTION.

The suggestion of the hypnotist can make believe the individual that he (hypnotist) it has had the effect of magnetic FINGERS.

It is therefore claim that hypnotic phenomenon attracting fingers in our favor; which, however, it would have occurred naturally. Mesmer suggestion is to persuade the subject to believe that the webbed fingers hypnotic phenomenon is due to him (hypnotist). At that time, the unconscious of the subject will give the hypnotist does not actually own power; only it thought so.

DIVERT THE SUGGESTION.

If the individual has managed to accept a fact, however, it would have occurred spontaneously or naturally UNION OF MAGNETIC FINGERS way (fingers sticking). So; if at that time synchronized by means of suggestion, that individual will be prepared to accept a slight deviation, thanks to the power that has given us unconsciously. If, feeling stick your fingers, you have agreed to close their eyes, convinced that I am the author of attraction, much more so accept, relax and sleep soundly.

IN SUMMARY:

We create a situation in which we know the psychological consequences.
We synchronized by means of suggestion.
And we avert our suggestion towards a certain goal.

1. - MAGNETIC FINGERS - STUCK FINGERS (SENSORY FAMILY)

This technique 1ra suggestion and induction of magnetic or webbed fingers are a "test Suggestibility" and a "Convincer" which has a strong physiological component, (organ function or body's natural response) and **SENSORY** "Suggestibility or Inductive Response Psychological that lets you create a situation, synchronize through suggestion and then divert it towards a certain goal.
Things to help us in our process of "Pre-Election / prehypnotic" to prepare and select the subject (patient or participant) who will work in our sessions or hypnosis

shows. If this technique of suggestion and induction of magnetic fingers or toes stuck is performed correctly, it will allow us to achieve three things:

1 suggestible properly preselect the candidate with whom we will start working on our therapeutic clinical hypnosis sessions or at our shows of street hypnosis or show.

2Subtly rid of people who are not interested in actually participating in our clinical sessions or hypnosis show; or prevent and detect those who try to challenge us, or are simply not yet ready to be hypnotized, but perhaps later be motivated to participate.

3 mentally prepare the subject with whom we will work, earn their trust, get into rapport with him, generate empathy and encourage you to participate actively and willingly, with an intention of positive purpose, which allows us to have an excellent session of therapeutic hypnosis or make a good show of show.

ALWAYS HAVE THIS BEFORE BEGINNING TO PERFORM YES-SET

Yes, in September: *A technique used to get put the subject on our side, and who agrees with us at least 3 "YES" followed ("covert orders").*

FOR EXAMPLE: *You can sit / stand "Yes", you can raise your legs / feet "Yes", you can take a deep breath "Yes". From that moment, it will be much simpler than your subconscious mind accesses our suggestions and inductions more freely, so it is ready to start the hypnotic process.*

Magnetic fingers "or" finger glued, explanation of the technique

This test can be performed individually or in groups and can make feet or sitting indifferently as prefer. In this exercise; what we will do is, the subject index fingers come together "stick together" like two magnets attract each other.

RECOMMENDATIONS: The first thing to do before making any covert test, test of suggestibility, convencers or deepening of states is the person explain in detail what is going to happen. That is to say; show the subject before beginning the exercise, which should do, and teach you how to do it ... as this gives us two advantages: 1st we suggest the subject and subtly prepared to think about what will happen. The 2nd we prevent the subject react or respond in the opposite manner to what we want to generate.

One way to do this would be something like: OK, let's try something interesting. A simple exercise to stimulate and empower your concentration. I would like you to put your hands in front of you in this way. (We placed us as reference what the subject will make your time)

We continue our explanation saying: Now you can entangle hands; palms together, fingers intertwined, crossed and thumbs, and well adjusted. (Again, we put our clasped hands as a reference of what the subject will do later)

We continue with the induction saying Now bend elbows like you're doing a prayer. (We bend our elbows, as a reference). I at this point; I always make a little joke, and tell the person in tone game that "you can do a prayer while you're there if you want" =). It's just a funny comment, that, used properly, allows us to eliminate stress or distraction in the person, and build rapport with the subject.

Then we continue with the explanation of the exercise, saying the following: Now put your index fingers in this way, in the up position, as if you held a gun. And then you shall separate as about 2 or 3 cm away, being in a "V". (We will put our fingers in the right position as reference what the subject will do later)

Once you reached this point; We continued explaining, telling her: Well now you concentrate, and you looked focused space between index fingers, look at your fingers and concentrate on them, because in a really moment and you feel like your fingers are going to get together, hugging and contact each other, as it would happen with two pairs of strong magnets, which are strongly attracted to each other. (We paste gesture and join the fingers to influence the person to do when you come to realize it). After the explanation, we asked the subject if he understood, and if he agrees to start performing the exercise with you now. If yes, we start exercising and ready.

Magnetic fingers "or" finger glued, Running Technique

The steps after explaining in detail the procedures to be followed by the subject to perform the exercise, as explained in the previous section ... Once; had done this part of the Yes Set and continue as follows:

1. What is italicized is the script of inductions and suggestions that we should tell the guy ... (2. What is in brackets () and bold italic are the instructions for the hypnotist) ... "3. The words continue in the normal format in quotes, "" are some additional instructions "...

> ***Yes, in September**: You can sit / stand "Yes", you can raise your legs / feet "Yes" now focus on exercise and follow all my instructions you agree, "Yes".*

Step 1 Ok, let's start, first, I want you to relax and take a deep breath, inhales and exhales, Inhale - Exhale, Inhale - Exhale. So is; right, you're doing fine. (Here we see that this following our instructions). Now I want you to put your hands in front of you in this way. (We placed us as reference what the subject should do, and you move both hands to the subject, as if we were placing them his hands in a correct position "This is just to make you think the hand position has some influence in the exercise ... Although in reality is a psychological placebo effect suggest it to think so "). Perfect; so, very well.

Step 2: We continue our explanation saying: Now you can entangle hands; palms together, fingers intertwined, crossed and thumbs, and well-adjusted. (Again, we put our clasped hands as a reference of what the subject will do)

Step 3: We continue with the induction saying Now bend elbows like you're doing a prayer. (We bend our elbows, as a reference). In this point; we can make a little joke, and tell the person in tone game "can make a prayer while you're there if you want" =). "This is just a fun statement, which allows us to eliminate stress or distraction in the person, and build rapport with the subject". "Once the person gets into possession of prayer, hands either clasped check with a gentle tug sideways, to ensure that is tight, this will insinuate the subject to keep the pressure in the course of exercise...

step 4: Then we continue with the explanation of the exercise, saying the following: Now put your index fingers in this way, in the up position, as if you held a gun. And then you shall separate as about 2 or 3 cm away, being in a "V". (We will put our fingers in the correct position, as a reference of what the subject should be doing with us)

step 5: Once you reached this point; We continued explaining, telling her: Well now you concentrate, and you looked focused space between index fingers, look at your fingers and concentrate on them, because in a really moment and you feel like your fingers are going to get together, hugging and contact each other, as it would happen with two pairs of strong magnets, which are strongly attracted to each other. (We paste gesture and join the fingers to influence the person and tell that's what was going to happen). "It is important to tell the subject to focus his gaze to the distance between his fingers, let it be absorbed by that distance, and imagine that had a strong magnet in each of his fingers"

> "This step is the most important because this is where we declare the subject order that your fingers will be approaching, and eventually these will end so close that it will be impossible unstick ... If we do this ... The goal was met. And we can terminate the exercise, as a test of suggestibility of Physiological Family "," If we take the exercise of Magnetic Fingers "or" sticky fingers to the next level we can move to the downrigger states and continue the exercise to move to state subject to the state Z1 Z2 "... This will explain later in steps 7 and 8

step 5: now started stick it, suggesting it as follows: Right well, once we have achieved, your fingers are attracted to each other, and now you can see and feel that they are stuck. Now I want you to imagine how your fingers begin to merge, join, stick tightly together, each other, Feel like those magnets stick together, like your fingers out a single piece of metal impossible to separate, the harder do to separate the fingers are stuck, the more you try to separate more and more stuck will, to the extent that for a few moments to stay melted, glued, inseparably connected to each other.

step 6: "At this point we begin to see how the fingertip of the subject began to hold together and glued attracted; and suggestion becomes increasingly evident and become increasingly clear, and we can feel the pressure that the person is exercising at that time we say try to separate it and will check that it is totally impossible "Once achieved the exercise correctly, we tell the person we're going to count from 1 to 3, and when we get to number 3 fingers can take off again, feeling completely liberated ... Now open your eyes. Bright it shows me that you can concentrate. "If the subject followed your instructions to the letter, it is impossible to separate the fingers, leaving hallucinated of your powers Hypnotic".

END OF YEAR

Important point *This technique of suggestion and induction is a test of suggestibility and a downrigger of hypnotic states and convicting according to the purpose it is made.*

In the first case, for example: If you use it as a Convincer or suggestibility test then you can apply this exercise at the beginning of the hypnosis session; or show, to evaluate and detect the degree of sugestionabilidad the subject (patient or participant). And correctly determine the degree of commitment that this person ... If at the end of the year; the person responded well to suggestions and paste your fingers and not able to open to the extent that we would Suggestion was, step by step, then it means that it is likely that the subject (patient or participant) is ready to enter the state Z1, which allow us to deepen the exercise and introduce it into the state Z1 ... Did you see how important are the suggestibility and Vinnie used?

In the second case, for example: If you use the exercise Magnetic Fingers "or" webbed fingers as some downrigger United hypnotics; then, to find that the person responded well to exercise, which has its fully glued fingers, and is deeply prepared to enter the Z1 state, then we could continue with two more steps ... In this case it would be Step 7 and Step 8; and would continue as follows, to deepen the hypnotic state and introduce more fully in the Z2 state.

<u>***step 7***</u>*: At this point we begin to see how the fingertip of the subject began to hold together and glued attracted; and suggestion becomes increasingly evident and become increasingly clear, and we can feel the pressure that the person is exercising at that time we say try to separate it and will check that it is totally impossible "Once achieved the exercise correctly, we deepen the state we tell the person: that's, that's, well, right. Note how they are starting to win your two fingers like a pair of strong magnets, each time they approach and stick and work more and more ... and as soon as you're sure your fingers are completely attached and attracted to each other, can afford Close your eyes and relax.* ***(As we say these inductions, we touch soft and subtly every part of the eye that we want the person relax (This allows the subject to remain concentrated and focused on the exercised; The same time we anchor them through touch "kinesthetic "the feeling of relaxation that we want to generate)),*** To follow the suggestion will continue to say: I want you to imagine now, as would be the muscles of your eyes so relaxed that just your eyes closed and feel your eyelids are completely closed, deeply closed, completely closed, only for a short time. That is, you're doing very well.

__*step 8*__*Now I want you to relax completely still, these muscles of your eyes, feel them completely relaxed, totally relaxed, deeply relaxed. (As we say these inductions, soft and subtle touch every part of the eye that we want the person relax).* Have great difficulty doing ... Your eyes are completely sealed, your eyelids are completely stuck ... Your eyelids can no longer raise your eyes and cannot be opened and, at times, despite all your efforts, will be impossible to raise your eyelids open and will be impossible for you to open your eyes ... Allow yourself to feel the muscles in your eyes constrict ... the more time passes more firmly stick your eyelids ... FROM NOW, When I say "three" your eyelids and your eyes will be completely closed ... as much as you strain yourself in lift, you will not make it ... as I say "three" will be impossible to open your eyes ... One 1 .... Your eyes are firmly closed ... Two 2 ... Your eyelids are getting more and more crowded ... THREE! Your eyelids remain stuck, your eyes are completely and totally sealed and fused ... That's right, once as your eyes are completely closed, your totally heavy-lidded and you are deeply relaxed (Here you approach the person and begin to rock her, moving slightly from side to the other, or back and forth to stimulate the feeling of deep relaxation and generate the "State of Trance Hypnotic Desire) and you order saying now, you walk into a deep sleep, sleep more and more deeply, you slip deeper and deeper into a deep hypnotic sleep ... now when I count to three you will relax even more, and you will sleep deeper and deeper still. 1 lose yourself relax 2, 3 sleep feel, Now sleep! once as your eyes are completely closed, your totally heavy-lidded and you are deeply relaxed (Here you approach the person and begin to rock her, moving slightly from side to the other, or back and forth to stimulate the feeling deep relaxation and generate the "State of Trance hypnotic Desire) and you order saying now, walk into a deep sleep, sleep more and more deeply, you slip deeper and deeper into a deep hypnotic sleep ... now when I count to three you will relax even more, and you will sleep deeper and deeper still. 1 lose yourself relax 2, 3 sleep feel, Now sleep! once as your eyes are completely closed, your totally heavy-lidded and you are deeply relaxed (Here you approach the person and begin to rock her, moving slightly from side to the other, or back and forth to stimulate the feeling deep relaxation and generate the "State of Trance hypnotic Desire) and you order saying now, walk into a deep sleep, sleep more and more deeply, you slip deeper and deeper into a deep hypnotic sleep ... now when I count to three you will relax even more, and you will sleep deeper and deeper still. 1 lose yourself relax 2, 3 sleep feels, now sleep! or back and forth to stimulate the feeling of deep relaxation and generate the "State of Trance Hypnotic Desire) and you order saying Now, walk into a deep sleep, sleep more and more deeply, you slip more and more deep into a deep hypnotic sleep ... now when I count to three you will relax even more, and you will sleep deeper and deeper still. 1 lose yourself relax 2, 3 sleep feels, now sleep! or back and forth to stimulate the feeling of deep relaxation and generate the "State of Trance Hypnotic Desire) and you order saying Now, walk into a deep sleep, sleep more and more deeply, you slip more and more deep into a deep hypnotic sleep ... now when I count to three you will relax even more, and you will sleep deeper and deeper still. 1 lose yourself relax 2, 3 sleep feels, now sleep!

Recommendations and final words: *To achieve better results, it is best to keep trying all the voices have been learning; until we begin to notice favorable and positive results, and the tone or volume of voice that suits are that we should use to stimulate the desired hypnotic trance states)*

****

"I never said it easy, but I promise you it will not be impossible ... You just have to be willing to pay the price of success and then enjoy the results the rest of his entire life." - YLICH TARAZONA. -

OBSERVATION OF INTEREST: 90% of people will do this exercise successfully. For that reason; You must hurry to put his fingers together quickly, as fast as 2 seconds and no more than 20 seconds. If they cannot do at this time, do something else. The reason that this test of suggestibility is so simple to do and is so successful in people. It is that the effect of moving fingers, they'll be allying without conscious effort, since it is a natural physiological reaction of the subject's hands. The physiological function that comes into play here is simple, as the tendons of the fingers are tight, causes the tendons in the index fingers move and come together, automatically allying with each other ... And that produces the hypnotic effect we want.

Although this exercise is simple and easy to recognize as a mental trick, if true, it may be. But also, it surprises you how much some individuals respond positively to this test. With open eyes, showing expressions and exclamations of surprise, that what you're saying, is actually happening.

IMPORTANT When this type of technique Sensory Family or any other exercise induction of this set are used, even if you know that the odds of success are in your favor. Your mindset as a hypnotist should be, you're doing this hypnotic phenomenon happen. Then you must be consistent, coherent and convincing in your approach. Remember your words, actions and thoughts will create the desired effect.

Another variation of this technique SENSORY family suggestibility test of magnetic HANDS. In this variation of the exercise we will join hands to your subject and attract them as if they were a pair of magnets.

1. - MAGNETIC HANDS - STUCK HANDS (FAMILY SENSORIAL)

This technique on the 2nd of suggestion and induction of magnetic or glued Hands, is a "test Suggestibility or Convincer" also has a strong physiological component, (organ function or body's natural response) and **SENSORY** *"Suggestibility or Inductive Response Psychological that lets you create a situation, synchronize through suggestion and then divert it towards a certain goal as we did in the previous year. If this technique of suggestion and magnetic induction hands or hands stuck is done correctly, it will also enable us to achieve three things:*

1 suggestible properly preselect the candidate with whom we will start working on our therapeutic clinical hypnosis sessions or at our shows of street hypnosis or show.

2Subtly rid of people who are not interested in actually participating in our clinical sessions or hypnosis show; or prevent and detect those who try to challenge us, or are simply not yet ready to be hypnotized, but perhaps later be motivated to participate.

3 mentally prepare the subject with whom we will work, earn their trust, get into rapport with him, generate empathy and encourage you to participate actively and willingly, with an intention of positive purpose, which allows us to have an excellent session of therapeutic hypnosis or make a good show of show.

ALWAYS HAVE THIS BEFORE BEGINNING TO PERFORM YES-SET

Yes, in September: *A technique used to get put the subject on our side, and who agrees with us at least 3 "YES" followed ("covert orders").*

FOR EXAMPLE: *You can sit / stand "Yes", you can raise your legs / feet "Yes", you can take a deep breath "Yes". From that moment, it will be much simpler than your subconscious mind accesses our suggestions and inductions more freely, so it is ready to start the hypnotic process.*

Magnetics hands "or" hands glued, Running Technique

This test can be performed individually or in groups and can make feet or sitting indifferently as prefer. In this exercise; what we will do is, that the subject's hands "come together" "stick together" and "attract" like two magnets attract each other mutually.

1 PART Now, in a moment I'll ask you to concentrate and put all your attention on what I say, like you did with your fingers. Only this time; I want you to use all the power of your imagination, because in a moment I will hold you close your eyes completely. But before closing my eyes, I'm going to ask you to put your hands in front of you in this way (we place as a reference of what the person should do, and you move both hands to the subject, as if we were placing them their hands in a correct position "This is just to make you think the hand position has some influence in the exercise ... Although in reality is a psychological placebo effect suggest it to think so"). Perfect; That is, here it is fine.

2 PARTS Now close your eyes completely, and imagine that you have two strong magnets attached to the palms, and these powerful magnets begin to come together and strongly attracted to each other. Now, you can give an embedded order and tell you: When you touch your two hands together, both your head and your two hands can relax and dropping forward, your hands and head, while you relax deeply.

3 PARTS: OK, now that you have your two hands in front of you, I want you to turn the power of your imagination, and you focus on the space between that between your two hands. I want you to imagine and the opportunity to have a clear idea of your hands allying each other and you can imagine and feel your hands stuck there.

4 Part Now close your eyes and imagine that these two powerful magnets that have attached to the palms of your hands are attracting magnetically and are trying to get together, get together and stick to each other. That's fine.

5 Part Go, feel, are already starting to come together now take the opportunity to imagine all the power of your imagination that the magnetic force between your two hands is getting stronger and stronger, the more and more close, more and more it becomes strong attraction of these powerful magnets to each other. Imagine that when children were playing with magnets and felt the magnetic attraction that united them, the beat, pulling your hooks to fully join them. I know I cannot tell you exactly when they will be touched, but I can assure you is going to play, they will unite and will attract one another, to touch each other.

5 Part Now when your two hands have touched, I want you to let your hands fall and your head fall forward onto your chest and relax deeply, completely, totally.

Here we can terminate the exercise we use as proof of suggestibility saying: Excellent. Now, you can open your eyes. You can also reinforce the exercise with a statement: You have a powerful imagination.

END OF YEAR

In this exercise, magnetic HANDS; like the above, I suggest that the hypnotist show exactly what the subject has to do and what will happen before asking the subject to do so. As this will give us two big advantages: 1st we suggest the subject and subtly prepared to think about what will happen. The 2nd we prevent the subject react or respond in the opposite manner to what we want to generate. Because remember that once we explained what will happen, and show how it has to do, it is likely that the subject will succeed in this exercise. even more so when they have gone through exercises magnetic fingers.

BRIEF EXPLANATION: Hands MAGNETIC logically are as magnetic fingers as you see; again, it is physiological components that come into play, causing those forces "Magnetic" making body parts (hands) to get together or appeal automatically, without conscious effort.

This technique MAGNETIC hands or hands has Paid bicomponent PHYSIOLOGICAL, and another component SENSORY ...
"1 Physiological" organ function or body's natural response
"2nd Sensorial" Inductive Response Suggestibility or Psychological
  ✓ **Create a situation** *of which we know the psychological consequences.*
  ✓ *It allows us to synchronize through suggestion.*
  ✓ *It allows us to divert suggestion towards a certain goal.*

POINT OF INTEREST This demonstration is intended to put the subject to imagine succeeding with exercise, displayed two strong magnets that attract your hands together, to ask them to concentrate and use their imagination to recreate that situation in mind. MAGNETIC HANDS exercise can be done with your eyes open. However, it is better if done with eyes closed. For that reason; We can begin by saying: This time I want you to really use the power of your imagination and your concentration, because in a moment I will hold you close your eyes completely. By saying this, you are giving the subject a reason to close his eyes. And this gives us the opportunity to observe how the person in question responds to our suggestions with your eyes closed. As this allows easier for them to use their imagination and concentrate better on exercise. Lie to us allows us to focus and observe closely, the subject's eyes for any signs of hypnosis, especially in REM, which then take advantage in our favor.

Test and Simulation Exercise "disguised test" Brief History and Explanation

This induction test or simulation exercise has been used for many years in the practice of hypnosis, especially in clinical therapy hypnosis; but also, sometimes it practiced as pre-trial shows of street hypnosis and shows like Simulation Exercise before the event. This covert test was one of the first simulated inductions I learned in my early days ... It was a quick learner and it worked superbly in practice. For that reason; I recommend it because it is ideal for the beginner hypnotist. Because it allows you to practice, rehearse and simulate the subject before making the "INDUCTION REAL". What it gives us a great advantage.

> *Personally, I have never failed to mesmerize with this simulated induction or disguised test. And I always use when I think, feel and see that it is appropriate.*

BRIEF EXPLANATION BEFORE APPLYING THE INDUCTION TEST OR EXERCISE

To begin this exercise, the first thing to do is explain to the person step by step, detailed and exactly what we are saying and doing. But above all; we must explain the subject, what effect it will have on them. always presents this covert Induction Test or simulation exercise teaching tone, as if you were trying to teach them something. Since, in this way, the conscious mind predisposed the subject to be paying attention, and prepare the unconscious mind of the person to receive covert orders and between the desired state of hypnotic trance.

This INDUCTION TEST or EXERCISE, there deferent variations that have evolved through the years. For this version we learn here in my book, use the technique to create a Test or Induction Simulation Exercise known as Catalepsy Arm. So literally, to achieve our purpose, rehearse and simulate the desired action with the person as often as necessary, to bring about the desired hypnotic phenomenon, it is time to realize the true INDUCTION, suggestion, convencers, disguised test or proof of suggestibility, downrigger states, among others.

The interesting thing about this powerful technique disguised test or exercise Induction Test and Simulation Exercise is performed correctly will produce the expected in the subject effects, before the person involved realize that we are inducing a hypnotic state desired. That is, that this technique may never get to make INDUCTION REAL. Since the subject will be hypnotized during one of the trials, hence the name.

Exercise Test or Simulation Exercise

This test unlike the above, it is recommended to be done individually and preferably make sitting (Although group and feet also works very well as long as the master very well, and above all know the technique and the goal you want achieved at the end). In this exercise or disguised test; what we will do is, that the subject's hands "relax" "entering cataleptic state" and "respond before our suggestions" as if obeying instructions and inductions we give them.

To begin, after explaining the intent of the exercise, and purpose to be achieved with the test or simulation. We begin with the art.

1 PART: Can I borrow your left arm ... What I do then is I'll take your left at your shoulder hand, and I will raise it in this way (In saying this, we take your hand? the subject by the subtle wrist and softly as we move towards the front and lifted her up, so that your left hand is suspended in the air in front of him and his elbow slightly bent at approximately 90 degrees to the height his shoulder in the shape, position where we want the person to respond to suggestion) ... Then continue: I do not want you to go into hypnosis yet, because first I want to explain this ... are you okay?

OK, ready, and to do this, it is vitally important because this action I am doing mu moving left hand up is something that will help you later to get into the desired state of hypnosis ... And then to go the hypnotic trance state, we just have to move your hand down this way. (In saying this we move your hand down in the initial position).

2 PARTS: You return to repeat the test or simulation, reminding the person what will happen soon; and tell you: Everything is going to notice the subject, it is that you'll get your wrist and raise and lower it in this way. (Also repeated the 1st half of the year, as it did at the beginning). For these two attempts, lift his wrist and then download them, speaking more softly, but still having a conversation at a normal pace.

3 PARTS: We continue saying: Now I'll talk to you in a certain way, (Modula's rhythm, rhythm and volume of your voice) and while the hand reaches a certain point, you'll notice a number of things that are happening inside you; that let you know you're going to get into hypnosis ... and (also repeated the 1st part of the exercise, as is the beginning we did). For three attempts, lift his wrist and ask her to close her eyes. And we continue with the induction saying now see and feel how slowly your eyelids begin to weigh yourself and that feeling will you begin to blink more and longer than usual, your eyes begin to feel and look more and more blurred, until when your eyes begin to close smoothly, change your breathing, your breathing will become increasingly more and more slowly, your heart rate will decrease slightly, and all those feelings together, you will go even encourage relaxed state still deeper and deeper, and that feeling will give peace and feel a comfort and tranquility all over your body .... Feels like rest, feel like you sleep, you feel like you're so relaxed ... relaxed (Here you approach the person and begin to rock her, moving slightly from side to the other, or back and forth to stimulate the feeling of relaxation deep and generate the "State of Trance Hypnotic Desire) Ok you're doing well, that's ... Now when you roll down your left arm again, you will return back to that state of deep hypnosis, and you're here with me fully awake ... If you understand nods, SI ok, ready then we will move your hand down this way and you will begin to awaken. Ok WAKE

4 Part: We continue with the induction saying: Now hear my voice, I will speak to you and tell you what you should do, as we have done previously, you agree (Modula's rhythm, rhythm and volume of your voice) here again (we repeat the 1 PART exercise, as they already have done previously). For this 4th attempt, got his left hand taken by the wrist and ask you as your hand up, and get up close your eyes. Then we continue with induction saying: Now I want you to get to experience the feeling of peace, comfort, tranquility ... Feel your eyelids again begin to weigh yourself and that feeling will you begin to blink more and longer than usual, your look began to feel and look more and more blurred, until you feel the desire to close your eyes gently, your breathing will change more and more relaxed, your breathing will become increasingly more and more slowly, your heart rate will decrease a little more and more, and all those feelings together, you will stimulate go even relaxed state still further and deeper, and that feeling will give peace and feel a comfort and tranquility all over your body .... I want you to allow yourself to feel like you rest, you feel like you sleep, you feel like you're so relaxed ... relaxed (Here you approach the person and begin to rock her, moving slightly from side to the other, or back and forth to stimulate the feeling of deep relaxation and generate the "State of Hypnotic Trance Desire) that is, you're doing fine, right ... well, that's what did very well ... Now when you roll down your left arm again, you will return back to that state of deep hypnosis, and you're here with me fully awake ... If you understand nods, yes OK, ready then we'll move your hand down this way and you will begin to awaken. Ok WAKE UP

5 Part but this time, let yourself go further and deeper, raise your hand NOW ... That's, well, you're getting, feels like as your left arm is raised you relax, you feel like as your arm up enter a state of peace and well-being and enter more and more into a deep hypnotic trance state, you probably notice that your eyelids weigh more and more, you will feel like your eyes are completely closed, that will be determined by yourself. I'm just going to help you relaxing more and more (Here you approach the person and begin to rock her, moving slightly from side to the other, or back and forth to stimulate the feeling of deep relaxation and generate the "State Hypnotic Trance Desire) Ok you're doing well, that's ... Now when I tell you lower your left arm, lower it and going back again back to that state of deep hypnosis, and you're here with me fully awake ... If you understand nods, yes OK, ready then move your left hand and lower it to and you will begin to awaken. Ok WAKE UP

As you could have noticed, every part I will add a few more steps, which are small details that go incorporating induction. By pacing and leading by the hand their experience through rapport, calibration, reframing and anchors. In other words, I point out what is happening (calibration) while ambiguously suggest what will happen (reframing) and is happening all the time, while search any signs of hypnosis (calibration) to be developed, so we can go building an action pattern (pacing) while I keep the conversation flowing and dynamic person (rapport) and through physical contact kinesthetic will generate stimuli and responses (anchors) ... finally allow me to take the person to the State of Trance Hypnotic wanted.

PART 6: However; to continue, if necessary, we can repeat the exercise again. If necessary repeat the exercise, all you have to do is repeat the previous step, it is we say (repeat Part 5 of the exercise, as it already did in step above) and ready ...

It is likely that the person, if you have successfully completed the Test or Exercise Simulation Exercise in the fourth or fifth time we have conducted covert testing, surely the subject began to raise and lower his left arm unconsciously. In other words, the person began to raise and lower the left arm alone, even before touching. What happens in these cases; is that when you rehearse or pretend a hypnotic phenomenon train the subconscious mind of the person to automatically answer your arm, hearing induction. And this is what you want, this is what we expect when we perform exercises tests or simulation exercises ... Build on the individual concerned the ability to play the hypnotic phenomenon that we are suggesting and bring it to enter the state Z1, the state Z2. When everything is done, the procedure correctly, what we do is to give the subject the minimum amount of stimulus, moving upward with your finger on the bottom of your wrist to stimulate the response, which is the rise in the arm ... While we concentrate on the development of exercise and pay attention to other signs that would indicate that the person is entering hypnosis, by realizing them, we make a downrigger state ... and deepen the person in the Z2 state and continue with another convicting.

ADDITIONAL RECOMMENDATIONS If your arm remains suspended in the air by itself, it is already the person has entered the cataleptic state of hypnotic trance and is among the states Z1 and Z2 ...

If on the contrary the left arm of the person has not kept entirely suspended ... We can keep repeating the exercise, an ideal way to do this and cause the arm catalepsy is that when we give the order to raise the arm, we help subtly upload.

One of the ways on how I do it is that even when going to release it, I tend to slowly release all fingers except the index finger is on the back of your wrist. This gives the message to the person that my hand still in his hand somehow, this will measure the degree or hypnotic level at which the subject is ...

If the person responds well, and leaves its suspended hand when subtly removed the index finger, then that means we have achieved our goal, and if on the contrary still feel that you need more suggestion to encourage him to reproduce the phenomenon itself, then you can simply repeat the exercise again if necessary. And you see how the person eventually end up entering the desired state of hypnotic trance, and hypnosis will have achieved its goal ...

FINAL WORDS

Good champions and champions "{(CONGRATULATIONS)}" and have reached the end of this book wonderful power of hypnosis in its special edition, with such dedication that I wrote for you. It was a long process of training and learning together you and I rode on this journey to your success and personal fulfillment.

This book will create and design thinking of you as a systematically INSTRUCTION MANUAL HANDY step; in order to go passing you by a mental process of continuous training learning through a "{(action pattern)}" well prepared and simplified to grant effective, optimal, effective, permanent results by the most powerful tools and methodologies modern hypnosis, TRANCE and PHENOMENA HYPNOTICS, Ericksonian hypnosis and Freudian suggestions and hypnotic inductions, HYPNOSIS CONVERSATIONAL, PATTERNS HYPNOTICS persuasive and SHOW hypnosis combined show with more advanced techniques and methodologies HYPNOSIS PSYCHOLINGUISTICS and PNL APPLIED (Neuro-Linguistic Programming).

Remember APPRENTICE, if you really want to deepen in this masterful art of hypnosis and hypnotism to higher levels ... invite you to read the full TRILOGY SERIES: PNL Applied Influence, Persuasion, suggestion and hypnosis - the Volume 2 and 3 where you will learn more inductions, Covert Tests, suggestibility and deepen, convincing United hypnotics with other advanced techniques and methodologies while at the same time teach you how to perform and create your own hypnotic exercises high level.

YOU IMAGINE all you can achieve getting to learn to master these techniques and advanced methodologies HYPNOSIS correctly. You can imagine how your life would change dramatically for the better, to be able to conquer all your dreams and goals you set out to achieve with hypnosis, thanks to these principles. NOW POSSIBLE!

WE SEE IN THE FOLLOWING BOOKS OF THE SERIES ...

Applied NLP, Influence, Persuasion, suggestion and hypnosis - Volumes 2 and 3

If you liked this book The Power of Hypnosis And you want to "help" with your contribution, to support me to continue doing this wonderful work, which, with love, prepared for you. You can do this through the following link or Link.

http://bit.ly/PaypalDonación
Thank you for your contribution

Well apprentice, after having finished reading my first book in the series: NLP Applied Influence, Persuasion, suggestion and hypnosis - Volume 1 of 3 "THE POWER OF HYPNOSIS" (Manual Theoretical and Practical Training in hypnosis, and Persuasive Skills Development Hypnotic), you can continue your training in hypnotism, ADVANCED HYPNOSIS and self-hypnosis.

APPRENTICE then invites you to read the two books ULTIMATE TRILOGY.

"PRACTICAL COURSE OF HYPNOSIS. How to hypnotize, anyone, Anytime, Anywhere ©-®...volume 2

"HYPNOSIS TO THE NEXT LEVEL. Advanced hypnotism, self-hypnosis, regression and Hypnotic Phenomena High Level ©-®. volume 3

Remember, take action and
MAKE THINGS HAPPEN
And start living a wonderful life
Principles centered with Standards
Highest of integrity and uprightness
And I promise that if you live these Rules
You and I soon see us in the
CUSP OF EXCELLENCE

Your great friend COACH YLICH TARAZONA

THE ROAD TO EXCELLENCE *"Alone; When you think big, when you think you can, when you have the conviction and certainty that you will achieve and you determine out of your comfort zone. And you start to persevere in your vision and mission of purpose, to achieve reach each and every one of your most cherished goals and put your plans into action firmly to go after your dreams and start believing in yourself. So is there; you started will enjoy the results have conquered your goals proposed before. "- YLICH TARAZONA. -*

MásterCoach.YlichTarazona@gmail.com
http://www.reingenieriamentalconpnl.com

ABOUT THE AUTHOR

PROFESSIONAL BACKGROUND:

Transformational Coach YLICH TARAZONA: Recognized Writer, Best-Seller Author, Speaker and High Level International Lecturer.

Expert in NLP or NEUROLINGUISTICS PROGRAMMING, Brain Reengineering, Mental Bioprogramming, Neuro Coaching, Persuasion and Hypnosis.

Considered in the different media as one of the most Outstanding and Influential Entrepreneurs within the field of MOTIVATIONAL NEUROSCIENCE and PERSONAL EXCELLENCE; destined to exercise a LEGACY in the lives of thousands of people, through its PASSION, ENTHUSIASM, DYNAMISM and PRINCIPLE-CENTERED LEADERSHIP.

Man, of FAITH and CHRISTIAN Convictions; focused on Principles and Values.

Founder of the portal MENTAL REENGINEERING WITH PNL ® - Virtual Community for Entrepreneurs. One of the Internet Website dedicated to providing COACHING in the CONSOLIDATION of Competencies and the Development of the Maximum Human Potential. Specialists in training, training and high-level training through Neurolinguistics Programming.

Creator of the PERSONAL COACHING SYSTEM in CEREBRAL REENGINEERING and MENTAL BIOPROGRAMMATION to reach goals, specify objectives and consolidate effective results of optimal performance; through a series of Audios, Podcasters, Tele-Seminars Online, Audio-Visual Workshops, Webminars and Magisterial Conferences of Presence.

Co-Creator and Re-Designer of the "NLP MODEL" and the effective formula "{(E - SMART - ER)}" [For the Establishment and Setting of GOALS, action plan and strategic planning principles to achieve and consolidate objectives].

Creator of WEBMINARS Audio Visual, TELE-SEMINAR Online and MASTER CONFERENCE [Re-Discovering Your Purpose and Life Mission].

Recognized "Author of the Series of BOOKS, Sequences of EBOOK'S and MASTER'S CONFERENCES" of [BRAIN REENGINEERING and MENTAL BIOPROGRAMMING © -®]. Among the most outstanding we have "How to Improve Your Self-esteem", "Free yourself from Internal Self-Sabotage", "Rediséñate and Reinvent your Life, Position your personal Brand or Personal Branding, Reengineering of Thought Processes among others.

Written by the **Master Coach YLICH TARAZONA**

Best-Seller Author of the series [THE MASTER CYCLES OF DUPLICATION AND MULTIPLICATION in the NETWORKS MARKETING, Universal Laws and Principles for Developing Your Multilevel Professional Business] Vol. 1, 2 and 3.

Creator of the INTEGRAL SYSTEM OF PERSONAL COACHING through NLP or NEUROLINGUISTICS PROGRAMMING to produce positive changes in thought patterns, and generate effective results of high performance and optimal performance, both individual and organizational level. This Offline and Online TRAINING SYSTEM has marked the lives of hundreds of entrepreneurs in person and has changed the mental paradigms of thousands of people worldwide via virtual. Inspiring those who participate, listen, see or read their teachings; to live extraordinarily focused on principles.

PURPOSE, MISSION AND PERSONAL VISION:

MY PURPOSE: To transmit to all my readers faith; and the strength to keep going, always with confidence and optimism despite the adversities. GUIDING THEM AS THEIR MENTOR AND PERSONAL COACH to find their life mission through a real opportunity for personal growth, to help them clarify their ideas, establish their goals, and develop a well-defined action plan, which will allow them to successfully conquer your most desired dreams. Allowing them to create their own future, writing the history of their own lives and forging their own destiny through a continuous cycle of tactics and strategies created for that purpose.

Similarly, I want to help my readers, trainees, participants and supporters to change negative thought patterns and limiting mindsets, teaching them to consolidate their skills and develop their maximum human potential.

MY MISSION: Becoming an instrument in God's hands, that allows me to impact the lives of hundreds, thousands and millions of people around the world.

Leave a mark that makes a difference in the lives of the people I teach and carry my message. And also leave them a legacy that transcends time. And let them evolve in all transcendental and important aspects of their lives, both personally, spiritually, emotionally as well as professionally, academically and financially.

MY VISION: Bringing people hope and an option that allows them to transform their lives for the better, to help them develop that seed of greatness we all carry within its interior, and encourage them to consolidate position and expand their maximum human potential, next level of success.

And finally, to establish a connection and empathy with all my readers, participants and supporters, to let me go climbing in the relationship with each of them, as far as possible. At the same time, I teach them to position and consolidate in all aspects of life in a balanced way ...

Helping them internalize the correct principles that allow them to reinvent itself, creating a new and improved version of themselves. Opening up new paths, new opportunities aperturandoles success, enabling them to lead their lives, to find himself on the road to transformation and personal excellence. And finally; resume more strongly, his path to success and personal excellence ...

OTHER PUBLICATIONS, SPECIAL EDITIONS, MINI COURSES, E-BOOK'S by the author

Hello such, my great friend reader, was a pleasure to have shared with you this time reading, I hope you enjoyed the most of the information in this book so lovingly prepared for you.

If you want to know some other of my works on Kindle from Amazon and CreateSpace I invite you to visit the following links. you great friend goodbye Coach YLICH TARAZONA

1.- *HOW TO IMPROVE YOUR SELF-ESTEEM.* Learn to program your mind and focus your thoughts to conquer everything that you propose in Life.
Amazon Kindle https://www.amazon.com/dp/B071NS4NPH
Paperback CreateSpace https://www.createspace.com/6763814

2.- *Liberate the self-sabotaging.* Learn to Strengthen Your Inner Warrior, Energy Balance your channels, control your emotions and direct your thoughts.
Amazon Kindle https://www.amazon.com/dp/B0716BWKR1
Paperback CreateSpace https://www.createspace.com/7120751

3.- *REDISÉÑATE and re YOUR LIFE.* The Art REDESIGN your life, REINVENT, REVIVE and create a new and improved version of yourself.
Amazon Kindle https://www.amazon.com/dp/B06XKCSTNZ
Paperback CreateSpace https://www.createspace.com/7195297

4.- *REDISCOVERING your life purpose.* Foundations for Living a Full Life, principle-centered and connected with Our Vision and Mission.
Amazon Kindle https://www.amazon.com/dp/B071FFVVM4
Paperback CreateSpace https://www.createspace.com/7195692

5.- *THE POWER OF GOALS.* Principles of Strategic Planning to achieve and consolidate your dreams and goals step by step.
Amazon Kindle https://www.amazon.com/dp/B071SF2QX7
Paperback CreateSpace https://www.createspace.com/6684686

6.- *POSITIONING YOUR BRAND PERSON.* Consolidate and establish your PERSONAL BRANDING in a competitive market through the "Love Brand".
Amazon Kindle https://www.createspace.com/6799772
Paperback CreateSpace https://www.createspace.com/6615804

*7.- NEURO-LINGUISTIC PROGRAMMING. **Practical Guide PNL COMPLETED - Modern Methodologies and Techniques for Effective Change Your Life**.*
Kindle Amazon https://www.amazon.com/dp/B072DVXBHR
Paperback CreateSpace https://www.createspace.com/7119256

*8.- The power of metaphors and figurative language. **Stories, parables, metaphors and allegories, Powerful Persuasive Communication Tools**.*
Amazon Kindle https://www.amazon.com/dp/B01ESBD7WY
Paperback CreateSpace https://www.createspace.com/6685297

*9.- Reengineering CEREBRAL AND REDESIGN OF THOUGHT. **Learn to reprogram Your Mental Processes and generate a Personal Reinvention**.*
Amazon Kindle https://www.amazon.com/dp/B0723BVN9G
Paperback CreateSpace https://www.createspace.com/6685293

*10-. THE POWER OF HYPNOSIS. **Theoretical and Practical Manual Training HYPNOSIS and Skills Development Hypnotic Persuasive**.*
Amazon Kindle https://www.amazon.com/dp/B076G97F14
Paperback CreateSpace https://www.createspace.com/7691037

*eleven-. PRACTICAL COURSE OF HYPNOSIS. **How to hypnotize, anyone, Anytime, Anywhere**.*
Amazon Kindle https://www.amazon.com/dp/B076G97F14
Paperback CreateSpace https://www.createspace.com/7691037

*12-. HYPNOSIS TO THE NEXT LEVEL. **Advanced hypnotism, self-hypnosis, regression and Hypnotic Phenomena High Level**.*
Amazon Kindle https://www.amazon.com/dp/B076G97F14
Paperback CreateSpace https://www.createspace.com/7691037
Coming soon...

*13-. THE BIG BOOK OF HYPNOSIS. **Hypnotism manual to learn hypnotize Anyone, Anytime, Anywhere**.*
Amazon Kindle https://www.amazon.com/dp/B076G97F14
Paperback CreateSpace https://www.createspace.com/7691037
Coming soon...

*14.- Multilevel marketing networks. **Masters Cycles of duplication and multiplication in the Network Marketing**.*
Amazon Kindle https://www.amazon.com/dp/B01IZTHD0M
Paperback CreateSpace https://www.createspace.com/6614144

15.- *PLANNING BUSINESS NOTEBOOK. Monthly Action Plan to Develop Your Business Successfully Multilevel professionally*.
Amazon Kindle https://www.amazon.com/dp/B01J1JEVHI
Paperback CreateSpace https://www.createspace.com/6612779

16.- *NETWORK MARKETING TO THE NEXT LEVEL. Universal principles to develop your MLM Project Successfully professionally*.
Amazon Kindle https://www.amazon.com/dp/B01MFDJNT9
Paperback CreateSpace https://www.createspace.com/6619923

17.- *MULTILEVEL MARKETING NETWORK. Network Marketing Business Opportunity Great XXI Century, Towards your financial freedom*.
Amazon Kindle https://www.amazon.com/dp/B01M5H4CG2
Paperback CreateSpace https://www.createspace.com/6669735

18. *WORDS AND PHRASES FAMOUS INSPIRATIONAL. Collection with more than 800 Thoughts and motivational quotes Leaders Largest in History*.
Amazon Kindle https://www.amazon.com/dp/B01J4MGSU0
Paperback CreateSpace https://www.createspace.com/6615169

19.- *PNL applied to communication. Patterns Persuasion, Conversational Hypnosis and Hypnotic Oratory, the Art of Persuasion, and Influence Others Positively*.
Amazon Kindle https://www.amazon.com/dp/B01MXT273E
Paperback CreateSpace https://www.createspace.com/6762851
Coming soon...

20.- *THE ART OF COACHING WITH NLP. Knowledge, Skills, Techniques, Coaching Practices and Strategies to achieve goals and achieve what thou meanest in the Living*.
Amazon Kindle https://www.amazon.com/dp/B01N1N49V8
Paperback CreateSpace https://www.createspace.com/6762787
Coming soon...

21.- *Reengineering MENTAL CEREBRAL and programming. A quantum leap in the evolution of SER - The New Era of Thought and The Awakening of Consciousness*.
Amazon Kindle https://www.amazon.com/dp/B01EQML2U4
Paperback CreateSpace https://tsw.createspace.com/6685305
Coming soon...

22.- *LAW AND UNIVERSAL PRINCIPLES OF SUCCESS.* **Biblical Principles for Success and Abundance Living in accordance with the Lord's Way**.
Amazon Kindle https://www.amazon.com/dp/B01MQQWLGT
Paperback CreateSpace https://www.createspace.com/6762826
Coming soon...

To acquire other display options and bought books on versions COVER TENDER STANDARD or PREMIUM HARDCOVER PROFESSIONAL WITH or WITHOUT FLAP, with or without cover, different qualities of prints (Black & White, Full Color, Ahuesada Premium Sheet) in Size pocket, American Printing or spiral ...

You can do it through my other official websites.

http://www.lulu.com/spotlight/Coach_YlichTarazona
http://www.autoreseditores.com/coach.ylich.tarazona

Continuous learning, continuous training and lifelong study are key among which we succeed, those who do not. - Ylich Tarazona. -

PUBLICATIONS EDITIONS BOOKS, E-BOOK AND SPECIAL REPORTS BY THE AUTHOR

OTHER PUBLICATIONS EDITIONS BOOKS, E-BOOK AND SPECIAL REPORTS BY THE AUTHOR

CONTINUING SERIES

WORKSHOPS, CONFERENCES, SEMINARS, COURSES MINI CREATED BY THE AUTHOR

FOLLOW THROUGH ALL OUR NETWORKS SOCIAL (SOCIAL MEDIA AND OFFICIAL WEBSITE)

Facebook, Twitter, YouTube, Google +, BlogSpot, Instagram, Pinterest, SlideShare, Speaker, LinkedIn, Skype and Gmail

https://www.amazon.com/Ylich-Eduard-Tarazona-Gil/e/B01INP4SU6
http://www.reingenieriamentalconpnl.com/
http://www.coachylichtarazona.com/

http://www.lulu.com/spotlight/Coach_YlichTarazona

http://www.autoreseditores.com/coach.ylich.tarazona

https://www.facebook.com/coachmaster.ylichtarazona

https://www.youtube.com/user/coachylichtarazona

https://plus.google.com/+ylichtarazona/posts

http://www.spreaker.com/user/ylich_tarazona

http://instagram.com/coach_ylich_tarazona/

https://www.pinterest.com/ylich_tarazona/

https://www.linkedin.com/in/ylichtarazona

http://es.slideshare.net/ylichtarazona

https://twitter.com/ylichtarazona

You can also contact the AUTHOR directly via e-mail by:
MasterCoach.YlichTarazona@gmail.com

Skype: Coaching_Empresarial

3rd Special Edition Revised and Updated by: Ylich Tarazona November 2017.
Design and Preparation of the Cover by: Ylich Tarazona
Kindle eBook ASIN: B076G97F14 / Kindle Soft Cover ASIN: 154997100X

ISBN-13: 978-1979740036
ISBN-10: 1979740038
SEAL: Independently Published ©

BISAC: Hypnotism / Hypnosis / Autohypnosis / Hypnotherapy / Hypnosis
The right of YLICH TARAZONA to be identified as the AUTHOR of this work has
been affirmed by SafeCreative.org, Registration Code: 1710184603711, in
accordance with Copyright Worldwide. Date: Oct 18, 2017